Guidelines for
Bias-Free Writing

BY MARILYN SCHWARTZ AND THE

TASK FORCE ON BIAS-FREE LANGUAGE OF THE

ASSOCIATION OF AMERICAN UNIVERSITY PRESSES

Guidelines for Bias-Free Writing

INDIANA UNIVERSITY PRESS

BLOOMINGTON • INDIANAPOLIS

The paper used in this publication meets the minimum re-quirements of American National Standard for Information Sciences—Permanence of Paper for Printed Library Materials, ANSI Z39.48-1984. ∞™

Manufactured in the United States of America

Library of Congress Cataloging-in-Publication Data
Schwartz, Marilyn.
Guidelines for bias-free writing / by Marilyn Schwartz and the Task Force on Bias-Free Language of the Association of American University Presses.
p. cm.
Includes bibliographical references and index.
ISBN 0-253-35102-2 — ISBN 0-253-20941-2 (pbk.)
1. English language—Usage—Handbooks, manuals, etc.
2. Learning and scholarship—Authorship—Handbooks, manuals, etc. 3. Discrimination—Language—Handbooks, manuals, etc. 4. Nonsexist language—Handbooks, manuals, etc. I. Association of American University Presses. Task Force on Bias-Free Language. II. Title.
PE1460.S474   1995
808'.027—dc20
  94-29281
    2 3 4 5 00 99 98 97 96 95

Contents

Preface

This book was prepared as part of the work of the Task Force on Bias-Free Language. Formed in 1987 by Carol Wallace Orr, then president of the Association of American University Presses, the Task Force was charged to promote bias-free usage—that is, writing free of discriminatory or disparaging language—in university press publications. Its work included educating the AAUP membership concerning bias-free usage, encouraging the development of press-level policies, and making practical resources on usage available to university presses.

Beginning in the early 1970s, many textbook publishers and professional associations of teachers, research scholars, and journalists adopted policies and guidelines concerning bias-free language. A survey of university presses conducted by the Task Force in 1988, however, indicated that scholarly publishing had lagged behind, particularly in the area of nonsexist usage. More than 85 percent of the two hundred respondents to a questionnaire devised by Carol Kasper and colleagues at the University of Chicago Press felt that gender-biased language occurs in scholarly publishing, and about 70 percent considered it a problem. Yet only a handful of presses reported having a policy regarding gender-free usage in their publications; most indicated that they relied on informal consensus and the discretion of authors and editors to avoid misleading and offensive language. At the same time, responses to the questionnaire reflected considerable disagreement about what constitutes gender-biased language and disclosed a great range of opinion concerning specific expressions and the appropriate criteria for accepting or avoiding them.

A survey of freelance editors employed by university presses, undertaken in 1990 by Julie Marvin with the assistance of Mary Lou Kenney and Marilyn Campbell, revealed similar findings about biased language in general. A substantial percentage of respondents stated that in editing scholarly writing they encountered such language frequently enough to consider it an issue in their work. Many rated the level of concern among university presses as lower than their own, perceiving the guidance from client presses as unclear and the support of editing to eliminate bias as indecisive. A majority indicated that they wanted more defined policies on usage and would welcome a handbook specifically addressing problems of biased language in scholarly writing.

This publication is an attempt to respond to that need and to give definition to the position statement adopted by the AAUP Board of Directors in November 1992:

> The Association of American University Presses urges its members to adopt a strong but flexible and intelligent

policy with regard to bias in language. Books that are on the cutting edge of scholarship should also be at the forefront in recognizing how language encodes prejudice. They should also be agents for change and the redress of past mistakes. Using words like *mankind* and *man* to refer to men and women, while convenient shorthand, embodies bias and introduces that bias into our perceptions of history and self. Use of the masculine singular pronoun (the "generic *he*") to refer to all people is misleading and exclusive. Insensitivity to racial and ethnic identities and to differences of religion, age, ability, and sexual orientation reinforces the conscious and unconscious attitudes that allow us too often to reproduce ignorance. The Association of American University Presses urges all of its members to adopt clear, sensible, formal policies to achieve a bias-free, inclusive language.

In formulating our recommendations, we surveyed a great many existing style guides, the most useful and readily available of which are listed in the bibliography. We also benefited from the support of other professional organizations and from the advice and examples (many cited in these pages) offered by individuals in university press publishing. Our guidelines were distributed in draft form to those who attended the 1991 AAUP national meeting, and copies of the draft were subsequently circulated to other interested individuals both within and outside the Association. Over the following year and a half, we assembled corrections, questions, and further examples from readers and users of the draft guidelines in an effort to refine our advice to scholarly and professional authors and to university press editors.

Many people have assisted us in completing our work. In addition to past members of the Task Force on Bias-Free Language, we owe special thanks to a great many individuals who have volunteered comments and criticisms. We are grateful for their contributions and of course take full responsibility for any errors and omissions—and any biases—that may remain. We ask readers to appreciate the difficulty of devising guidelines for bias-free usage without being overly prescriptive or resorting to politically expedient or trendy solutions inappropriate in scholarly writing. We also hope readers will understand the impossibility of being truly comprehensive or entirely up-to-date in such a publication, when new terms and topics constantly demand recognition, and advice in areas of rapidly changing and hotly contested usage may quickly be superseded. We welcome comments and emendations that may be taken into account in any future editions of these guidelines.

Finally, we realize—lest there be any misunderstanding about this—that there is no such thing as truly bias-free language and that our advice is inevitably shaped by our own point of view—that of white, North American (specifically U.S.), feminist publishing professionals.

Some authors and editors will not accept all of our recommendations, but we hope that this exploration of issues will help them make informed, thoughtful choices. We recognize that context and genre, as well as individual style and preference, will influence those choices, as indeed they should. Our aim is simply to encourage sensitivity to usages that may be imprecise, misleading, and needlessly offensive.

Task Force on Bias-Free Language
June 1994

Past and Present Members:

Marilyn Schwartz (chair)   Julie Marvin
Carole Appel   Norma Mikkelsen
John Bergez   Mary Murrell
Marilyn Campbell   Carol Orr
Holly Carver   Mary Pasti
Susan Fernandez   Karen Reeds
LeAnn Fields   Lee Campbell Sioles
John Gallman   Seetha Srinivasan
Carol Kasper   Ellen Stein
Mary Louise Kenney   Annette Windhorn
Elizabeth Makowski

Guidelines for
Bias-Free Writing

1

Gender

Introduction

1.1 Authors and editors may never entirely agree among themselves or with each other about specific points of nonsexist usage. No matter. What is important is that they share an in-principle desire for clear, precise writing that is free of unwarranted bias. The following recommendations are not intended as prescriptive; their purpose is to encourage sensitivity and common sense. Nonsexist writing is never simply a matter of using or avoiding specific expressions. Particular choices must always be made in context—the author's meaning and tone, the subject matter, the readers' level of understanding—and will inevitably be guided by an individual's taste and literary voice.

Gender-Neutral and Nonsexist Language

1.2 *Gender-neutral* describes language formally unmarked for gender—*police officer* and *flight attendant,* for example, as contrasted with the marked terms *policeman* and *steward-*

ess. Nonsexist refers to language that avoids gender stereotyping. Although gender-neutral language is often recommended as a means of avoiding sexism, gender-specific
language is not necessarily sexist. The following passage
from a university press book employs the marked *women
teachers,* the courtesy title *Mrs.,* and the strongly connota-
tive *lady*—usages often proscribed in guidelines for nonsexist writing—to make a specific point about the
influence of certain *women* (as opposed to *men*) teachers
on the author's life and to characterize the manners of
pre-1919 gender debate in the United States:

> My great women teachers in high school were suffragists.
> They transmitted the feminist message. One of them, Mrs.
> Gray, my English teacher, told the story of the gentle lady
> who invited a gentleman to have tea with her. In the
> course of the afternoon the conversation turned to the
> suffrage movement. "How absurd," the gentleman said.
> "Think of your cook voting." To which she replied sweetly,
> "Yes, I often do. You see, he does."

Conversely, gender-neutral terms may conceal a sexist
bias. In an article published in the *Canadian Review of
Sociology and Anthropology* (1985) under the title
"Humanity's Propensity for Warfare," the use of the gender-neutral terms *humanity* (in the title) and *humans* instead of *man* is in keeping with the recommendations of
many guidelines for nonsexist usage. But in the following
excerpt the focus of the discussion implicitly narrows
from *human* aggression to warfare *among males* as the
author summarizes a study of "intergroup warfare" in a
society where one objective of such conflict is the acqui-
sition of females. The author neglects to comment on this

shift or to qualify the applicability of such a study to any generalizations about humanity:

> Do ritualized aggression and lethal conflict serve similar functions among humans? Alcock . . . concludes that most threatening or violent disputes are employed to resolve contested ownership over scarce or potentially limiting resources. . . . Sociologist Van den Berghe . . . interprets intergroup warfare as a rational means of gaining livestock, women, and slaves, gaining or keeping territory, or gaining, controlling, and exploiting new territory.

The portrait of the teacher, although employing gender-marked and semantically loaded terms, is nonsexist; the passage on warfare, possibly cloaking an underlying androcentrism in gender-neutral language, may be sexist. It is certainly unclear and misleading.

Generic Man *and Its Compounds*

> **Example 1:** "No recent book has better portrayed the common man in China."—From a review of *The Autobiography of a Chinese Working Woman*

MAN

1.3 In traditional usage the term *man* means both "adult male human being" and "human being." The former definition renders the use of the latter, generic meaning imprecise or incongruous, even in contexts where the author is clearly referring to the human species. As substantial philosophical and linguistic research shows, whereas *man* may be understood as generic in such contexts, it is not interpreted as gender-neutral: readers think of the representative of the species as male. The typically bemused reaction to the following illustrates:

> Man, like other mammals, breast feeds his young.

Besides such incongruities, generic *man* can foster ambiguity. In Example 1, readers may rightly wonder whether the woman's autobiography yields special insights about ordinary men or about women and men equally under the rubric *common man.*

1.4   Because of the ambiguity caused by overlapping generic and gender-specific meanings of the word, writers sometimes slip unconsciously from one into the other, as a memorable example cited by Frank and Treichler (1989: 189) shows:

> The central issue in man's evolution was bipedalism. When man thrust himself erect, he truly became *Homo erectus:* for he discovered front-to-front copulation. And woman in her turn was rewarded by orgasm, unknown to all other species.

1.5   Many alternatives are available to those who seek to avoid such inequities, incongruities, ambiguities, and unintentional lapses, among them terms such as *humanity, hu-*

mankind, humans, human beings, human species, people, and first-person plural pronouns (*we, us, our, ours*).

> **Example 2:** "If we are to defend our beliefs . . . we must ask the most fundamental questions that can be asked: questions about the nature of man, his relationships to other men, and his place in the universe."—From a university press book

1.6 Because of the present confusion between the two meanings of *man,* writers who restrict the use of the term to its gender-specific sense sometimes need to signal that they are doing so, for example by employing the terms *male* and *female* frequently, introducing the parallel sex-specific *woman* early in the discussion, and using appropriate sex-specific pronouns.

> **Example 3:** A prospective reader may rightly wonder about the subject and scope of a university press book entitled *America's Working Man: Work, Home, and Politics among Blue-Collar Property Owners.* The author acknowledges a debt to "the men and their wives" who were interviewed and observed, yet the publisher's description and the blurbs characterize the book as a study of "blue-collar workers."

COMPOUNDS WITH *MAN*

1.7   Compound forms employing *man*—for example, *man-power, manmade, craftsman, chairman, congressman,* and *fire-man*—are likewise imprecise or ambiguous when they refer to both sexes or to a person of unspecified sex. Usage guidelines recommend gender-neutral alternatives, and many state and federal agencies in the United States have officially adopted unmarked terms—*personnel* or *human resources, manufactured* or *artificial, artisan, chair* or *chairperson, member of Congress* or *representative,* and *fire fighter*—especially for occupational titles.

1.8   Some writers and editors find particular alternatives unacceptably newfangled or unnecessarily freighted with feminist intentions, as in the often-targeted *chairperson.* Critics of language change sometimes even caricature such terms, as in the proposed *personhole cover* for *manhole cover* and (based on pseudo-etymology) *personfactured* for *manufactured.* The resources listed in the Bibliography include many excellent glossaries and thesauruses that offer a selection of legitimate gender-neutral alternatives—even for *manhole cover* and for the difficult mid-position compounds such as *sportsmanship*—among which may be found choices acceptable to nearly every individual taste.

> **Example 4:** "She's a very craftsmanlike sort of person."—From a university press editor's description of an author's writing skill

PERSON AND *PEOPLE, PERSONS*

1.9   The terms *person* (singular) and *people* (plural) may replace generic *man* in references to individuals and to aggregates of the population:

> A man without faith is lost.
> A person without faith is lost.
>
> Man abandoned the farm for the city.
> People abandoned the farm for the city.

But these terms cannot always substitute for generic *man,* and *people* carries an indefinite connotation unsatisfactory in some contexts:

> Man had not yet learned to reason.
> A person had not yet learned to reason.
> People had not yet learned to reason.

In such cases, other revisions may be preferable:

> Humans had not yet learned to reason.
> We had not yet learned to reason.

1.10   Writers and editors occasionally object to compounds with *person* and *people*—for example, *chairperson, ombudsperson, craftspeople, laypeople*—as neologisms. To be sure, some of these forms are of recent vintage; others, however, have long histories, duly recorded in the *Oxford English Dictionary,* which individuals are encouraged to consult before rejecting this class of words wholesale.

Other alternatives may be found for terms that offend the individual taste.

1.11 Whereas the plural *people* indicates a group or aggregate, the plural form *persons* designates a collection of individuals and is often used interchangeably with the former term. Compounds with *persons* may be newly minted or well established in usage; writers should consult a dictionary for accepted forms but exercise caution in employing terms of very recent vintage recorded by the newer, descriptively based dictionaries.

FALSE PARALLELS

1.12 Usage guidelines recommend that gender-neutral occupational titles replace their corresponding gender-specific compounds with *man* and *woman*. Yet in some contexts gender specification is relevant or is necessary to avoid ambiguity and is therefore appropriate. In such cases, writers need to ensure that gender-specific terms are correctly paired: *chairman/chairwoman,* not *chairman/chairperson* or *chairman/woman chairman.*

Personal Pronouns

GENERIC *HE*

1.13 A widespread convention of English grammar prescribes that the pronoun *he* (or *him, himself, his*) be used when its singular antecedent of unspecified gender refers to a group that includes both sexes:

> An editor should present his changes in the form of suggestions subject to the author's approval.

This convention is also invoked when the antecedent is one of the indefinite pronouns—for example, *each, every, anyone, everyone*—which are grammatically singular:

> Everyone has a right to his own opinion.

Those following these practices—including usage experts, prescriptive grammarians, and many editors, scholars, and professional writers—often consider them fundamental to correct English and defend them on the grounds of grammatical tradition and stylistic grace.

1.14 But notions of correct English are not immutable: consider, for instance, the now-accepted use of *none* with a plural verb. Nor is the inclusive use of masculine pronouns inscribed on clay tablets "the way God intended them," as one university press author asserted to his editor. Generic *he* was not widely taught as a "rule" of grammar until the nineteenth century, and it then supplanted a much older grammatical tradition employing the common-gender *they* (or *them, themself, their, theirs*) in the singular, as in Shakespeare's

> God send everyone their heart's desire

—an alternative usage that, despite generations of grammatical instruction, persists, in colloquial speech, in such sentences as

> Everyone has a right to their own opinion.

1.15   Strict adherence to generic *he* results in incongruities and
ambiguities. In the first example that follows, a sort of
"multiple choice" construction, the masculine pronoun
seems illogical because one of the specific antecedents is
female; in the second example, cited by Frank and
Treichler (1989: 147), the pronoun is unclear because we
cannot be sure whether it is being used in the generic or
gender-specific sense:

> Bruce and Jane divorced because each wanted to focus
> on his own life.

> Dryden's reader is more than just a compromise of
> Dryden's tastes and prejudices; he also represents a class
> of intellects and has an intangible aesthetic life.

1.16   Even when readers understand that *he* is being used in
the generic sense, they think of the referent as male.
Writers may inadvertently slide from the generic to the
gender-specific sense of *he,* as in another example quoted
by Frank and Treichler (1989: 153) from a 1975 psychol-
ogy textbook:

> The depressed person often becomes aware of strong feel-
> ings of self-dislike; he feels worthless and guilty about his
> shortcomings. He believes that nothing he can do will
> alleviate his conditions. . . . Crying spells may set in, the
> person loses weight, finds himself unable to go to
> sleep. . . . Food no longer tastes good, sex is not arousing,
> and people, even his wife and children, become wholly
> uninteresting.

1.17 In violation of the "rules" concerning generic *he, she* often appears in contexts where cultural gender expectations influence the choice of grammatical gender:

> A nurse must undergo rigorous training before she is licensed.

COMMON ALTERNATIVES TO GENERIC *HE*

1.18 The problems associated with generic *he* undermine its utility as a generic. Many alternatives exist that are within the boundaries of prescriptive grammar and consistent with standards for good writing. Some are quite simple; others require special skill in revision. All demand good judgment and sensitivity to context: mechanical changes may sacrifice the meaning, character, or style of the original, and successful revision often involves a combination of techniques.

1.18.1 *Revision in the plural.* Recasting a statement in the plural is often the simplest way to avoid generic *he:*

> In the occasional awkward situation where the lower-ranking individual feels the difference is too great to permit first-naming, he tends not to address his superior directly.

> In the occasional awkward situation where lower-ranking individuals feel the difference is too great to permit first-naming, they tend not to address their superiors directly.

In some contexts, however, revision in the plural may blur the specificity of a passage:

> The newspaper vendor, for example, does not take a reverent stance in his dealings with the professor when he comes for his *New York Times,* especially if he makes more money than the professor.

> Newspaper vendors, for example, do not take a reverent stance in their dealings with professors when they come for their *New York Times,* especially if they make more money than the professors.

If such revisions are unsatisfactory, the author or editor may need to resort to one or more other techniques instead.

1.18.2 *Substitution of* he or she, he/she, s/he, he (she), (s)he. A double-pronoun construction can be substituted for *he.* The forms using slashes or parentheses, although appropriate in some legal, technical, and official contexts, are generally deplored as stylistic abominations. *He or she* (some prefer to reverse the customary order to *she or he* at least half the time) is acceptable, although it may seem cumbersome, particularly if it is repeated:

> In the occasional awkward situation where the lower-ranking individual feels the difference is too great to permit first-naming, he or she tends not to address his or her superior directly.

Using the double pronoun may be preferable to recasting

a statement in the plural when it is important to preserve a focus on particularity. It may also be desirable if the author wishes to emphasize the presence of women in an activity or field from which they have been excluded. But the device should be used sparingly to avoid obtrusive repetition.

1.18.3 *Elimination of the pronoun.* In the preceding example "a superior," rather than "his or her superior," would eliminate the repetition of the double-pronoun construction. In many cases the generic pronoun can simply be omitted or the definite or indefinite article (*the, a, an*) substituted:

> An editor should present changes in the form of suggestions.

> Everyone has a right to an opinion.

1.18.4 *Restructuring.* Other sentences may require more radical restructuring to eliminate the personal pronoun. The writer or editor may, for example, employ a participial phrase (constructed on the *-ing* form of the verb) or a gender-neutral relative pronoun (*who, whoever*), as in the following revision of a previous example:

> The newspaper vendor does not take a reverent stance in dealing with the professor who comes for a *New York Times,* especially if the vendor makes more money than the professor.

1.18.5 *Repetition of the noun or substitution of a synonym.* This last example also illustrates noun repetition ("the vendor"), another technique for replacing generic *he*. A second example combines the substitution of a synonym with other revisions:

> The educated and self-conscious Indian anthropologist is aware of one dimension of his present that only he can be aware of, because this awareness arises out of the intolerance, resentment, and defensiveness he feels about it.

> Only the educated and self-conscious Indian anthropologist is aware of one dimension of India's present, because this awareness arises out of the indigenous scholar's feelings of intolerance, resentment, and defensiveness about it.

1.18.6   *Shift to first person* (I, we, us), *second person* (you), *or impersonal third person* (one). The sentence in Example 3—

> A prospective reader may rightly wonder about the subject and scope of a 1984 university press book

—could entangle a writer in subsequent *he*'s because of the unmarked singular antecedent *reader*. But a writer can choose another form of address, provided it is consistent with the tone of the passage. First- and second-person forms sound familiar and conversational and may be used in informal writing:

> We may rightly wonder about the subject and scope of a 1984 university press book.

> You may rightly wonder about the subject and scope of a 1984 university press book.

We identifies the writer with the reader; *you* addresses the reader directly. With these pronouns, however, a writer must take care not to presume an identity with or consensus among readers (e.g., "We recognize that we have been socialized to defer to male authority") or to suggest an invidious distinction ("You people . . . ").

> **Example 5:** "Why do we fear a woman who merely takes the initiative in satisfying her sexual appetite? The answer partly appears to be that we are built that way."—From a university press manuscript

The impersonal third-person is more formal:

> One may rightly wonder about the subject and scope of a 1984 university press book.

A shift to the impersonal third person may, however, produce a flotilla of *one's*—or a reversion to third-person masculine forms in an unconscious attempt to avoid such congestion:

> Corruption exists when one illicitly puts one's own interests above those of the people and ideals one is pledged to serve.

> Corruption exists when one illicitly puts his own interests above those of the people and ideals he is pledged to serve.

As these unsatisfactory revisions illustrate, *one* is best used sparingly, and writers should avoid mid-sentence shifts in point of view.

1.18.7 *Alternation of masculine and feminine pronouns.* In some passages a judicious alternation of gender pronouns is effective and serves to emphasize the presence of women where generic *he* renders them invisible:

> The employer must ask a number of questions about every candidate. Does she have strong references? Does he have relevant experience?

Special care must be taken to avoid illogical alternation of pronouns or the distribution of gender pronouns in a sex-stereotyped fashion:

> Can she type? Can he drive?

Alternating third-person pronouns by chapter—*she* in one chapter, *he* in the next—may sometimes provide a readable solution to generic *he*, although it does not work in many situations.

1.18.8 *Singular* they. The inadequacies of generic *he* and the persistence in informal writing and speech of singular *they*, despite its proscription in formal written English, argue for tolerating this once widely accepted usage in specific colloquial contexts. Some linguists recommend this form within prescribed grammatical boundaries, such as to specify an indefinite pronoun or a "multiple choice" antecedent:

> Everyone has to carry their own luggage.

> Bruce and Jane divorced because each wanted to focus on their own life.

Although many scholarly and professional writers and editors have been educated to avoid singular *they* as substandard, it is now endorsed by some authorities, among them the *American Heritage Dictionary of the English Language,* 3d ed. (1992), which notes that it "may be the only sensible choice in informal style," and the *Chicago Manual of Style,* 14th ed. (1993). We urge its acceptance in informal writing in grammatical constructions such as the above.

Example 6: "Every person who parks here does so at their own risk."—Sign at parking lot entrance, Barclay's Bank, London

---

1.18.9 *Use of passive voice.* Recasting a sentence in the passive voice can be a simple means of avoiding generic *he.*

> It is difficult for the South Asian to overestimate the importance of history, so omnipresent is change on the subcontinent. . . . He can achieve an understanding of himself,

> his family, subculture, social phenomena, and naggingly
> intense contradictions and confusions only through history.

> It is difficult for the South Asian to overestimate the
> importance of history, so omnipresent is change on the
> subcontinent. . . . Only through history can an under-
> standing of self, family, subculture, social phenomena,
> and naggingly intense contradictions and confusions be
> achieved.

But the result can be wordy and awkward, as style guides
unequivocally state in recommending the active voice as
more forceful and direct in writing. Passive constructions
should be employed sparingly and only when more concise, elegant alternatives to generic *he* are unavailable.

1.19   The acrobatic revisions sometimes required to avoid generic *he* may deter some writers and editors. So may the
occasionally strained results. To be sure, what might seem
awkward at first may sound more natural, and finally
correct, with repeated use. At the same time, skill, sensitivity to context, and good judgment are necessary to
avoid distorting the meaning of a passage or altering the
style and character of the original. Revisions should not
introduce stylistic flaws, such as the blurred focus, repetition, or wordiness that may be caused by overuse of
plural forms or double-pronoun and passive constructions. Authors and editors should also avoid inconsistent
and incongruous corrections:

> If the body heat of the female (or male) is increased by
> only two or three degrees, its song goes one semitone

higher, and the partner no longer answers: he no longer recognizes in her (or in him) a possible sexual mate.

They should likewise avoid needless correction (hyper-correction) of appropriately used sex-specific pronouns:

> Everyone should be able to decide for himself or herself whether to have an abortion.

ANTHROPOMORPHIC PRONOUNS

1.20 Writers commonly use the masculine pronoun *he* for an animal unless it is identifiable as female—or unless it is a cat, to which "feminine" characteristics are sometimes ascribed. The underlying assumption that the male is the norm, or representative, of a species is particularly evident in field guides and natural histories that apply nonparallel labels to the sexes, such as *cardinal* and *female cardinal.* Observations of (presumed) males of a species, as well as captions accompanying illustrations, may in addition characterize animals in gender-stereotyped human terms ("A stallion guards his brood of mares"). The neuter *it* is recommended unless the sex of an animal is identified, in which case the appropriate gender-specific pronoun can be used; sexist characterizations of animal traits and behaviors are inappropriate.

1.21 The feminine pronoun *she* is still used by some authors to designate countries and ships (possibly tracing back to the gender of the Latin nouns *patria* and *navis*). Cities, storms (hurricanes, for instance), and abstract entities such as nature are also assigned feminine pronouns. Such usages are quaint at best, and because they may lure writers into ascribing "feminine" characteristics (whether positive or negative), they should be avoided. *It* is preferred.

1.22   Although some writers accept the neuter *it*, as an alternative to *he*, for infants and very young children of unspecified sex, many individuals find this alternative unacceptably dehumanizing. Other terms should be employed or the passage rewritten:

> The baby reached out his (*or* its) hand.

> The baby reached out a hand.

GENERIC *SHE*

1.23   *She* (or *her, herself, hers*) is traditionally used when the antecedent is clearly female. Some scholarly and professional writers now also use *she* in a generic sense, specifically to challenge the convention of generic *he:*

> The economic metaphor says that the agent faced with a bribe makes a calculation. She trades off the potential benefits of accepting the bribe and undertaking a corrupt act against the potential costs of doing so.

Some readers may find this usage exhilarating; others may perceive it as bizarre or confusing or may interpret it as reverse-sexist. The device can be effective when it clearly contests cultural gender expectations. That is, in subjects and traditions of discourse where *he* has been universally employed and men are assumed to be present, it may temporarily redress the traditional omission of women. It may also be effective when used in a specific context as a rhetorical device to make a point. Except for these specific purposes, which are achieved at the risk of distracting or antagonizing readers, authors should seek gender-inclusive expressions.

Gender-Marked Terms

FEMININE SUFFIXES

1.24 Most English agent-nouns, that is, nouns signifying the performer of an action, have a common-gender form applicable to both sexes: *aviator, doctor, usher.* The addition of feminine suffixes such as *-trix, -ess,* and *-ette* causes the common-gender form to acquire a predominantly masculine sense, while the feminine form—*aviatrix, doctoress, usherette*—becomes an auxiliary term. As linguistic studies have demonstrated, in such masculine/feminine pairings the feminine form often takes on a trivializing or pejorative connotation: *poet/poetess, master/mistress.* Forms designating women of a particular race, ethnicity, or religion are offensive: *Negress, Jewess, Quakeress.*

> **Example 7:** "Like many midwives, Mrs. Ballard was also a locally renowned nurse and doctoress, so she encountered doctors in many medical situations outside the birthing room."—From a university press manuscript

> **Example 8:** "There was a black woman flyer—
> an aviatrix named Miss Bessie Coleman—who
> had excited people in general, not only be-
> cause she was a woman who could fly, but
> also because she was black."—From a university
> press manuscript

1.25   Although titles of nobility (*princess, duchess, countess*) are un-
likely to change, authors are encouraged to employ the
common-gender agent-nouns rather than feminine variants
in most other cases. The preference for these standard forms
is reinforced by professional associations, institutions, and
businesses, as well as by government agencies: many women
who perform in the theater call themselves *actors* rather than
actresses, and professional acting guilds are beginning to reflect
this usage; the Episcopal church calls women ministers *priests,*
not *priestesses;* the U.S. government's dictionary of occupational titles lists *farmer* but not *farmerette;* many restaurants
employ *waiters* or *servers* (of both sexes) rather than *waiters*
and *waitresses*—ungainly forms such as *waitron* and *waitperson*
are entirely unnecessary.

1.26   Writers must resort to gender-neutral alternatives where the
common-gender form has become strongly marked as masculine, for instance, *flight attendant* instead of *steward/stew-
ardess.*   The glossaries and thesauruses included in the
references at the end of this book list a range of gender-neutral alternatives from which to choose. Writers need not
resort to terms unacceptable to the individual taste.

1.27 Feminine inflections on imported words. Some words derived from French continue to receive feminine inflections in English when referring to women: *blond/blonde, brunet/brunette, divorcé/divorcée, fiancé/fiancée, protégé/ protégée.* Some usage manuals recommend that the masculine forms be adopted for common-gender usage whenever possible. This suggestion seems acceptable for designations of hair color and complexion, particularly if writers limit the words to the adjectival use (*blond hair, brunet complexion*)—a practice advisable in any case to avoid the reductionism of identifying a person (often a woman) solely by this feature (*a blonde, a brunette*). The use of the masculine form as a common-gender word, however, has yet to gain widespread acceptance by scholarly and professional writers in the other instances cited above. Writers should in any case be sensitive to the potentially disparaging connotations of the feminine forms and should avoid faulty parallelisms (*a blonde/a man with blond hair, a divorcée/a divorced man*) that reinforce negative stereotypes. The Latin *alumnus/alumna* (*alumni/alumnae*)— both masculine and feminine forms are inflected for gender—are not objectionable; guidelines suggest *alums, graduates,* or *former students* for mixed-sex references.

Example 9: "In 1986 National again followed the example of USX (*née* U.S. Steel), choosing a new name: National Intergroup."—From a university press manuscript

GENDER EPITHETS

1.28   The adjectival use of *girl* and *lady*—as in *girl reporter, lady lawyer, woman writer*—is generally discouraged because of the trivializing connotations of these words and the implication that the agent (*reporter, lawyer, writer*) is male unless otherwise specified. The adjectives *male/female* and *man/woman* are acceptable only if sex is a variable necessary to the discussion. The expression *male nurse,* employed gratuitously, is as sexist as *woman doctor;* but either is appropriate in a context in which gender specification is relevant:

> This book discloses important new insights about gender roles and gender relations by looking at what happens when women and men enter nontraditional occupations. It concludes that there are some important differences between the experience of female marines and male nurses.

> I would prefer to have a woman doctor.

1.29   Where writers need to specify gender, they should observe correct parallelism of terms and should in particular avoid pairing *woman* with *male.* The use of *male/female* is often restricted to technical, demographic, biological, medical, and legal contexts, and *man/woman* employed in other contexts.

Example 10: "We had a secretary to the board, Mr. Holsey, as well as two or three lady secretaries who took dictation."—From a university press manuscript

---

> **Example 11:** "Urban planners and farm wives
> . . . shared similar images of the automobile as
> liberator."—From a university press manuscript

Idioms, Proverbs, Figures of Speech, and Allusions

1.30   Writers often employ set phrases, figures of speech, and
allusions, including many cast in language now considered sexist—*old wives' tales, mother nature, maiden name, he
who hesitates is lost, things are in the saddle and ride mankind.*
Some style guides recommend revising such expressions
or substituting gender-neutral alternatives. We cannot
endorse a wholesale purging of these traditional English
expressions and rhetorical devices. To be sure, sensitive
writers are likely to abandon such overtly sexist phrases
as *old wives' tales* in favor of alternatives like *folklore* and
superstition. They may avoid other expressions as sentimental (*mother nature*), quaint (*maiden name,* now commonly replaced by *family name* or *birth name*), or
hackneyed (*he who hesitates . . .*).

> **Example 12:** "Men of letters and poets may
> equally belong to the fraternity of heroes."
> —From a university press manuscript

1.31   It is not necessary to eschew traditional technical terms, such as *feminine rhyme* (in poetry) or *masculine ending* (in music), which refer to, or derive from analogy to, the inflections of grammatical gender. Writers should exercise care, however, to avoid introducing gender stereotypes— e.g., "weak" rhymes and "strong" endings—into discussions employing such terms.

1.32   In the same vein, writers need to be sensitive to the inappropriate or trivial use of metaphorical language referring to sexual experience or sexual violation:

> This is the virgin forest, where the hand of man has never set foot.

> The already weakened Environmental Protection Agency was raped by the Reagan administration.

The first example is a badly mixed metaphor by any standards; the second, employing an image of extreme personal violation to convey a sense of political disempowerment, is questionable—one need only substitute the word *castrated* to understand the possible excess of connotation.

1.33   Rather than eradicating set expressions and gender-specific figurative and allusive language altogether, however, writers need to consider context and tone in determining their suitability. The conventional characterization of important scholarship as seminal ("of, relating to, or consisting of seed or semen") might seem innocuous in praising Perry Miller's *Errand into the Wilderness* but incongruous in describing a gender study by a feminist scholar:

> I believe she has made an important contribution, indeed a seminal one, to the study of sex roles and gender behavior.

Similarly, an allusion such as that to Emerson's historically resonant phrase "things are in the saddle" might nicely fit a passage about U.S. social and industrial change in the nineteenth century but seem out of place in a discussion of twentieth-century patterns of female immigration. When invoking such a reference, a sensitive writer also considers whether knowledgeable readers are likely to recognize the origins of the gender-specific language without a disclaiming phrase ("in Emerson's words") or "scare quotes" around the imported expression—distancing devices that may be employed sparingly in some circumstances.

Syntactic Constructions

AGENCY

1.34 Cultural gender expectations may affect language at the deeper level of semantic and syntactic choices attributing active agency to men and passivity to women. The following sentence, from a biographical sketch of the typographer Beatrice Warde, illustrates:

> The marriage did not last. Frederic stayed on the Continent to design books, and Beatrice, retaining her married name, eventually settled in England.

Whereas the man is described as acting purposefully ("stayed . . . to design"), the subject of the narrative is not accorded parallel self-determination in the development of her career ("settled"). Similarly, in a collection of letters between two distinguished literati, Bernard Berenson and Clotilde Marghieri,

> readers . . . discover how, thanks to her friendship and correspondence with Berenson, Clotilde Marghieri became one of Italy's most perceptive and insightful novelists.

1.35   Passive voice verbs, in particular, may deny female agency. When an editor asked a university press author whether he needed to qualify a statement that there had been "progress" in rational notions of justice regarding women, the author responded:

> That she [the editor], as a woman, has been granted (presumably) a university education speaks to the point.

Example ¶3: "Husbands kill their wives much more for suspected infidelity and feared desertion than for any other reason. Interestingly, police files show that many women contribute to their own demise by taunting their husbands, boasting of their new lovers, attacking their husbands' sexuality, or threatening to leave."—From a university press manuscript

---

1.36 Conversely, semantic and syntactic choices may unjustly attribute responsibility or agency ("blame the victim"):

> Lucretia's beauty appears to have led one of her Inquisitors astray.

ORDER OF PAIRS

1.37 In many expressions referring to both sexes, the male term is traditionally placed first: *male and female, men and women, he and she.* Although there are several possible linguistic explanations for this phenomenon, as well as some obvious exceptions (*ladies and gentlemen,* used primarily in direct address), this ordering may reflect a semantic hierarchy also exhibited in other set pairs—*good and bad, great and small—* or may connote a hegemony. Some writers prefer to reverse the traditional order in such fixed expressions: *female and male, women and men, she and he.*

The Default Assumption and Faulty Parallelism

> **Example 14:** "However buffeted a Jew might feel in the course of his daily existence, on the Sabbath he was king in his house, meant to be, on that day, a haven of peace and joy."— From a university press manuscript
>
> **Example 15:** "The skilled Ford auto worker and his wife who works in a cafeteria have sufficient family resources between them to satisfy all conceivable average wishes."—From a university press manuscript

1.38   Writers may unconsciously assume that the referent of a gender-neutral noun is male. This "default assumption" is sometimes revealed in a disconcerting shift to gender-specific language in mid-passage:

> Southerners have too many bass to catch, deer to stalk, girls to chase, automobiles to race, and beers to drink to spend time reading.

1.39   The default assumption may also be disclosed by faulty parallelism, in which a gender-neutral term is paired with one marked as feminine. In the following newspaper report, the writer assumes that a doctor is ipso facto male, although a reader might reasonably ask whether one woman or two were killed:

> An army doctor and a woman serving as a medical specialist were killed this morning by mines as they tried to assist in taking Iraqi prisoners.

1.40   Scholars are especially sensitive to the intellectual pitfalls of the default assumption in defining research problems and drawing conclusions: a demographic study of "immigrants and their wives" is flawed in conception; conclusions about "blue-collar workers" based on interviews with working-class men may be overgeneralized.

Example 16: "Older women in classical head-to-toe chadors sometimes come by, but so do businessmen and fashionably dressed women who look like they just interrupted a shopping trip."—From a university press manuscript

---

Naming

1.41   *Courtesy titles.* Most guidelines for nonsexist usage urge
writers to avoid gratuitous references to the marital status
of women, including the courtesy titles *Miss* and *Mrs.*
Scholars normally refer to individuals solely by their full
or their last names, omitting courtesy titles, even those
that do not identify marital status—*Mr.* is usually super-
fluous and *Ms.* may seem anachronistic or ironic if used
for a woman who lived prior to the second U.S. feminist
movement of the 1960s (*Ms. Emma Goldman, Ms. Lola
Montez*). Historical figures and literary characters traditionally known by their courtesy titles—for example, *Mrs.
Thrale, Mrs. Malaprop*—should, of course, be designated
according to convention, unless, in a writer's judgment,
a special rhetorical purpose is served by departing from
it. If using courtesy titles, as, for example, in prefaces and
acknowledgments, a writer may employ those that carry
no information about marital status (*Ms.* and *Mr.*) or retain
only professional titles, such as *Dr., Rev.,* and *Professor.* A
writer should nonetheless honor individual preferences
if known: some married women request *Mrs.;* others employ *Miss* with their professional name, regardless of their
marital status; still others deplore *Ms.* because of its feminist connotations. Because African American women
have had to struggle for the use of traditional courtesy
titles, some prefer *Mrs.* and *Miss;* if so, a writer should
preserve these titles even in contexts where they would
normally be omitted altogether.

1.42   *First-naming.* Careful writers normally avoid referring to a woman by her first name alone because of the trivializing or condescending effect: *Emily* (for *Emily Dickinson*), *Margaret* (for *Margaret Thatcher*). To be sure, some women are known only, or chiefly, by a first name and may be so designated: *Cleopatra, (Queen) Elizabeth*. In biographies and other writing about related individuals, it is acceptable to refer to women and men by their first names provided usage is parallel and referents are clear: *Virginia and Leonard (Woolf), William, Henry, and Alice (James)*. References to nobility must follow custom, notwithstanding these guidelines—*Lord Byron, Lady Caroline*.

1.43   *Parallelism.* Except for the special circumstances noted above, women's and men's names should receive parallel treatment with respect to the use or omission of courtesy titles and the form (full names, first or last names only). Writers should avoid asymmetrical usages such as a discussion of *Virginia* and *Woolf* or *Freud* and *Anna*, or acknowledgments to (the colleague) *John Smith* and (the typist) *Mrs. Jane Jones*.

History and Patriarchal Traditions and Cultures

1.44   Gender-specific language should not be changed to suggest that women are included in all-male activities and experiences, past or present. Overzealous revision for inclusive language is a special risk in history and in studies of patriarchal traditions and cultures. Careful writers will, of course, verify the scholarly accuracy of gender-marked terms before employing them: masculine nouns and pronouns would be misleading in a discussion of the chiefs of certain prehistorical Caribbean Indian peoples, because both women and men held the position of chief; the term *medicine man* would be inappropriate in a culture with both female and male shamans. Gender-specific language would be more precise for advertising professionals in the early twentieth-century United States, because the advertising profession at that time was almost exclusively male. Writers need to clarify their terminology if readers may find it ambiguous:

> Although a small minority of women played a role in shaping the content of national advertising, as described in Chapter 2, I have occasionally resorted to the phrase *advertising men* to epitomize the profession. Despite its generic inaccuracy, this gender-specific phrase does provide an occasional reminder of the overwhelmingly male dominance of the process of creating and approving advertisements. It also dramatizes an important aspect of the social context in which the ads of the 1920s and 1930s must be understood. As I explain in detail in Chapter 3, the advertisements of this era were generally perceived by their creators as communications from a rational and therefore putatively masculine elite to the emotional, "feminine" masses.

1.45   A scholarly writer's attention to issues of gender-specific language may in fact make an analysis more precise:

> The problem of masculine and feminine pronouns has bothered me all through the writing of this manuscript. To use "he or she" as the unmarked pronoun in every

instance seemed intolerably cumbersome. To opt for "he" everywhere seemed repugnant to my political sensibilities and also false to the current state of the language, where, increasingly, efforts are being made to give "she" equal time. It also seems clear to me that in contexts where "he" most often would so occur in this book (referring back to "the philosopher," "the poet," "the good agent"), its presence is far from being really unmarked: it does encourage the imagination to picture the character in question as male. Nor is this an irrelevant concern in writing about this material [Greek tragedy and philosophy]. For the tragedians all have a claim to be taken seriously as thinkers about the privileges and the moral status of women; in each of the plays that we shall discuss, a woman defends her claim to moral and political equality. Plato has a good claim to be called the first feminist philosopher—though his position is more radical still: for it is the denial that the body, therefore gender, is of any ethical significance at all. He is also the first thinker I know who pointed out that feminism ought to lead to changes in unmarked linguistic gender. At *Republic* 540c, Socrates expresses concern that Glaucon's failure to use both masculine and feminine participles, when referring to the rulers, may give rise to the false impression that they are talking only about males. Aristotle's conspicuous anti-feminism is an issue that we shall discuss. My first idea, as I considered these questions, was to adopt the completely arbitrary "solution" of using "he" as unmarked in even-numbered chapters, "she" in odd. But this proved distracting and harsh to readers of widely varying political beliefs. Nor, clearly, was it a solution that the natural language could ever adopt. I therefore decided, on reflection, to follow Plato's practice in the above-mentioned passage, by using "he or she" fairly frequently, in order to remind the reader not to think of men only, but reverting (as Plato does) to the masculine in between, in order to avoid cumbersome sentence rhythms. I have also been sensitive to the context—since there is no use pretending that "he or she" is appropriate when speaking of an Aristotelian ruler as imagined by Aristotle; whereas there is great use in employing this form for Plato.

1.46   The gender-specific language that some religions use to refer to deity may be appropriate in a discussion of religious traditions. Such language, too, may warrant explanation or comment from an author. A writer may choose gender-marked language to describe the beliefs of a patriarchal religion but employ gender-neutral terms to analyze them.

Quoting and Paraphrasing

1.47   Direct quotations should not be altered in scholarly writing. This injunction poses a special dilemma for writers who quote sources containing sexist language. Especially if an author is striving for nonsexist prose, such quotations may be confusing or distracting.

1.48   *Warning labels and evasions.* Some scholarly authors insert *sic* ("thus") in square brackets following sexist words in direct quotations, but this device may be distracting, especially if repeated. If it is employed, an author often needs to flag only the first instance to alert readers:

> It is the dissolution of Ego boundaries that gives the hypnotist his [*sic*] apparent "power"; because his "commands" do not operate as something reaching the subject from

the outside, demanding submissiveness. To the subject
they are his own thoughts and goals, a part of himself.

A judicious use of ellipses or bracketed interpolations may
enable an author to skirt the problem—provided this
technique does not falsify the sense or tone of the original:

> By "culture" we mean those historically created selective
> processes which channel men's reactions both to internal
> and to external stimuli.

> . . . which channel . . . reactions both to internal and to
> external stimuli.

> . . . which channel [our] reactions both to internal and to
> external stimuli.

In particularly egregious cases, direct quotation may be
unnecessary, and paraphrase with proper attribution may,
in the writer's judgment, be sufficient.

1.49 *Prefeminist sources.* Warning labels, elisions, and bracketed
substitutions in quotations predating contemporary standards of nonsexist usage are gauche. Educated readers
will not find the gender-specific language in Pope's "Essay
on Man" objectionable. They may, however, wonder
whether, in using *man,* the poet meant to include
women—or even thought about the question.

1.50 *Clarification of gender-specific terminology.* An author may
simply quote gender-specific language because suppress-
ing or flagging it would be ahistorical or would mangle

the original. In such cases, the sense of this language in the context of the quotation should be clarified. How are readers to interpret the statements of an eighteenth-century poet about "man"?—part of the scholarly writer's responsibility is to explain the terms under analysis.

1.51 *The voice of the commentator.* Besides quoting gender-specific language without comment, an author sometimes echoes the language of the source being discussed. Whereas male generic usage may be appropriate in the historical context of a quotation, by replicating the language in paraphrase or commentary an author may introduce confusion. In the following passage, the writer picks up Rousseau's use of generic *man*—while passing over the quoted gender-neutral plural *people* without explanation—and finally alights on plural *men:*

> "The first language of man," [Rousseau] says, "the most universal, the most energetic language, and the only one he needed before it became necessary to persuade men in an assembly, is the cry of Nature." In those early days "people spoke only in poetry." Man had not yet learned to reason, but that was fine, since his life was an unspoiled vision of simplicity and his needs were few. . . . Love, hate, pity, anger are the things that first raised men's voices.

A conscious analytic distance between the language of the source and the voice of the commentator is essential. Some writers explain the relationship between them in a note:

> I have deliberately used "men" or "man" in this essay when it seems clear that the thinkers whose works I am describing eliminated women from consideration as par-

ticipants in government, even though women often ex-
ercised informal political influence.

Here, the writer's attention to male generics in quotations
and to her own linguistic choices has led her to recognize
an important limitation in the theories of the authors
being discussed.

Scholarly Apparatus

ACKNOWLEDGMENTS

1.52 An author's thanks, however personal and heartfelt,
should not stereotype or trivialize the contributions of
women to the finished work. Most readers are familiar
with the rounds of applause for the diligent (sometimes
female) typist, the nurturing or fanatically tidy (sometimes female) editor, and, in books by male authors, the
supportive spouse:

> As for [the wife of one of the authors], we remain amazed
> that she could put up with the intensity and frequent
> weariness of two [scholars] at their work, and we thank
> her for all her support, all the errands she ran for us, all
> the much-needed cups of coffee.

In a previously mentioned study of "America's working
man" (Ex. 3), the author's gratitude to "the men and their
wives" who made his research "so enjoyable" causes the
reader to wonder whether the women as well as the men
were observed and interviewed or merely served the
author beer in the living room.

DISCLAIMERS

1.53   Disclaimers concerning sexist language are not recommended as an alternative to revision. They ask readers, in effect, to disregard (or mentally translate) the text, and they do not address the serious problems of inequity, imprecision, and ambiguity that sexist usage creates. Disclaimers are often full of specious reasoning:

> A technical matter of diction requires mention here, namely my unwillingness to supplement masculine pronouns with feminine ones. Various devices for coping with the problem have been tried elsewhere with embarrassing results, for the reason that they violate the law of parsimony, omnipotent in science and art. Any statement becomes unreadable when it contains differentiations not relevant to the proposition. No writer would say, "He bites the left or right hand that feeds him." Now that the masculine pronouns, which have always been "unmarked," as the linguists say, are in the process of becoming marked, we can expect our language to supply us soon with terms that embrace both genders equally. In the meantime, an author who would not know how to discriminate against women should be permitted to obey the demands of his trade.

In another context this same author humorously observes that "dogs differ more from one another than do ladies"— an ad hominem rebuttal, to be sure.

BIBLIOGRAPHIC CITATIONS

1.54   Important scholarly contributions by women should be duly recognized and cited; the imputed neglect of such scholarship is an issue beyond the scope of these guidelines. But when writers seek to document sources by women scholars, they are sometimes confounded by name-changing practices. Many women—and some men—follow the custom of changing their name upon marriage or divorce; in addition, some feminist scholars adopt one or more "movement" names and may publish over time or simultaneously (often in different contexts) under several of them.

1.55   Some women, of course, do not change their name upon marriage or continue to use their birth name for publication and other professional activities. Some adopt a hyphenated surname consisting of a birth name and the husband's family name, in which case consecutive bibliographic entries will identify an individual as the author of works under the several nomenclatures. If a woman has published under her husband's family name and later returns to her birth name or adopts a feminist name, however, a scholar may employ *see* or *see also* cross references in bibliographic entries. Likewise, citations of works by a woman publishing under several names may be cross referenced.

1.56   Some women scholars use only their initials with their surname, as a matter of custom (a widespread practice on the Continent and in the UK) or in an effort to avoid gender bias. Writers should exercise care in assuming that scholars are male unless a given name suggests otherwise.

> **Example 17:** "According to Peterson . . . the Antarctic treaty was possible because the alternative, scrambling for territory and attempting to defend it, was regarded by all parties as being a less desirable alternative than the treaty. But his examination of the process does not lend much hope that nations will be able to deal easily with other international disputes."—From a review of a book by M. J. Peterson

INDEXES

1.57 Indexers of scholarly works must accurately reflect content while avoiding analytic categories that merely reflect gender assumptions. They also need to anticipate the interests of other scholars whose research on women and gender can be assisted by careful indexing of relevant topics.

> **Example 18:**
> "Women. See Betrothal gifts; Concubinage; Dowry; Exogamy; Family; Footbinding; Marriage institutions; Widow chastity
> "*Wu* (nonbeing), 144"
> —From the index to a university press book

Translations, Reprints, Collections of Documents

1.58 Translators must exercise careful judgment in rendering a text in English. They need to consider the readership and the purpose of the translation—whether it be simply to render the ideas or also to reflect stylistic or cultural nuances—before determining whether gender-biased characteristics of the original warrant replication in English. Translators should avoid recasting gender-neutral into sexist language, as in some biblical translations.

1.59 When publishers reprint old or classic texts or issue collections of historical and literary documents, they need to consider whether these publications contain sexist or other offensive language that will undermine their value and usefulness. Educated readers generally understand that scholarly publishers may not revise the language in a reprinted text, a costly and complex process, unless the text is intended for classroom use in the primary or secondary grades. Scholars normally do not sanction tampering with the wording of original documents. In such special cases a publisher or academic editor should include a disclaimer in the foreword, preface, or introduction that provides a context for the dated language.

2

Race, Ethnicity, Citizenship and Nationality, and Religion

Race and Ethnicity

2.1 The word *race* refers to a category of people identified on the basis of similar visible physical characteristics—sometimes characteristics perceived by the writer but having no scientific basis. Because even scientists disagree about the criteria for defining specific races, the term should be avoided or used cautiously.

2.2 An *ethnic group* is broadly defined as a group with which individuals are identified, or with which they identify themselves, on the basis of cultural characteristics. Every person has one or more ethnic origins, although not all individuals identify themselves strongly or consistently with an ethnic group. In writing about a multicultural society, authors should take care not to imply that ethnic groups are defined by their departure from some spurious norm—to imply, that is, that *ethnic* means "not of the mainstream." Not all minority groups are ethnic, and not all ethnic groups are minorities. The term *ethnic* is an adjective; the noun forms (*an ethnic, ethnics*) may be considered offensive.

2.3   The term *minority,* often applied to an ethnic group or to people of color, should be used with caution. A "minority" may be defined not on the basis of population size, color, or ethnicity (e.g., women and people with disabilities are sometimes described as minorities), but in terms of power in a particular society or on the basis of participation in special programs (e.g., scholarships for minorities, recruitment programs). Writers should bear in mind that ethnic groups and people of color are not numerical minorities in many societies, and whites are a minority in the world population.

Citizenship and Nationality

2.4   The word *citizenship* refers to legal status as a member of a particular nation. *Nationality* may be used to mean either citizenship or ethnic origin; it may therefore be ambiguous in some contexts. In general, writers are urged to be alert to changes in place names resulting from shifting political boundaries, and they should exercise care in using contemporary place names for regions when writing about a period that predates the establishment of current national borders or should employ the historically accurate alternatives:

The president expressed concern about the economic status of the former USSR.

The story concerns the lives of early settlers in what is now Montana.

Writers should also note territorial and ethnic disputes over externally imposed borders when selecting and defining geographical designations.

2.5   Besides nuances of citizenship, nationality, and political identity, writers need to be sensitive to derogatory regional designations (e.g., *hick, hillbilly, Okie, redneck, city slicker*).

Religion

2.6   Not all belief systems are religions. They should be described rather than pigeon-holed. Even within the context of organized religions, there are ranges of beliefs and practices as well as factional differences among practitioners, such as Orthodox, Conservative, and Reform Jews, liberal and conservative Baptists, and Sunni and Shiite Muslims. Terms may be pejorative rather than descriptive in some contexts—*born-again, cult, evangelical, fundamentalist, sect*—or may be disparaging popularizations—e.g., *Moonie* for a member of the Unification Church. Writers should be sensitive to religious issues in wording, such as "the Prophet says" or "Allah says," rather than "Muhammad says," for discussions of the Quran; the more inclusive *place of worship* rather than the Christian-centered *church;* the distinction between *Sunday* and *Sabbath*.

Preferred Designations

2.7   Styles and preferences for designating peoples and groups change over time and differ from region to region. Members of a particular group may disagree about the preferred designation even at a given time or may use a term among themselves that they would consider offensive if used by a nonmember. Sensitive writers will attempt to designate people by the terms they prefer, although research may be required to ascertain the most acceptable current language. As a general rule, authors can avoid giving needless offense by replacing overly broad categories with more specific terms. Gratuitous references to an individual's ethnicity or group identity are inappropriate.

Hyphenated Identities

2.8   Many usage guidelines and published works represent a person with a specific ethnic identity as a "hyphenated" citizen: *an Italian-Canadian, a Chinese-American.* Some people object to the hyphenation of these terms on the grounds that they characterize such a person as less fully a member of the society than an "unhyphenated" person. Our recommendation is to omit the hyphen except in expressions where the first term is not a free-standing prefix (*Anglo-American*), unless members of a group prefer a hyphenated form.

2.9   If individuals are identified by origin or ancestry, writers should employ parallel language (e.g., *European American,*

Japanese American) to avoid implying that the unqualified term denotes some implicit norm (e.g., *American*—a problematic word, in any case, to North Americans outside the United States—to mean "of western European or English ancestry").

Ethnocentrism

2.10   As the preceding paragraph suggests, language can imply a norm by which groups and peoples are measured, e.g., *nonwhite, non-Christian*. Some common expressions, such as *flesh-colored* (for pink or beige), are inherently biased.

> **Example 19:** "Commercially prepared canvases were sold in white as well as light grey, pink, and flesh color."—From a university press manuscript
>
> **Example 20:** "The drama of deeply blue children assuming a normal pink color after the operation . . . created a sensation."—From a university press manuscript

2.11   The "default assumption," an unspecified, often unconscious, norm (for example, white), is sometimes manifested in asymmetrical pairings, such as "two men and a black woman." Also, first-person plural pronouns and adjectives (*we/us, ours, our*) may in some contexts convey the assumption that all readers share the author's racial, ethnic, or national identity.

> **Example 21:** "The element of frontiering individualism that is so historically distinctive in the American condition has endowed our artists and thinkers with a positive valuation of risk and exploration that sets them off from the European backdrop of our settlement and ancestry."—From a university press manuscript

2.12   More subtle is language deriving from what might be characterized, for the Western Hemisphere, as the *discovery myth*, the implicit assumption that lands, peoples, and cultures did not exist prior to the arrival of Europeans—*Old World, New World, Columbus discovered America, the first settlers came by wagon train.* Many writers prefer *nonliterate* to *illiterate* to describe a culture without a writing system, and some anthropologists prefer the term *consultant* to *informant.*

> **Example 22:** "Man is not so much determined by the world he inhabits as the crucial determinant of that world. His impact upon his environment is most striking when he moves into new, previously uninhabited areas and comes into direct—and usually violent—contact with less advanced groups."—From a university press manuscript

*Set Expressions, Color Symbolism, Historical
Allusions, Similes and Metaphors*

2.13   Most scholarly and professional writers assiduously avoid
stereotyping—the Jewish mother, the British stiff upper
lip, the inscrutable Japanese, the stoic American Indian.
They may be less aware of the many common English
expressions that originate in a disparaging characterization of a particular group or people—*Siamese twins,
Chinaman's chance, Dutch treat, Mexican standoff, Indian giver,
to gyp* (from gypsy), *to jew, to shanghai, to get one's Irish up.*
Even some long-accepted common names for botanical
species—Niggerhead Cactus, Digger Pine (from a derogatory name for California native peoples who used the nuts
from the *Pinus sabiniana*)—are offensive and are now
undergoing revision in the scientific community.

2.14   Color symbolism, particularly of black and white, suffuses
the English language—*to blacken* (defame), *black-hearted*
(malevolent), *white* (pure) *as snow.* Such symbolism in
English surely predates contemporary instances of racism,
and it would be undesirable, indeed impossible, to erad-
icate such symbolism entirely; nevertheless, writers
should be sensitive to contexts in which it may be offensive. Likewise, authors should be conscious of contexts
in which some historical allusions, similes, and metaphors may be offensive or unintentionally humorous, and
especially conscious of the trivial application of terms
heavily freighted with historical and emotional associations—*he worked like a slave to become the first African
American to graduate at the top of his class.*

Example 23: "Reagan and Weinberg tried to welsh on the defense cuts."—From a university press manuscript

Example 24: "Among the many new proposals is the incorporation of 'bio-rational insecticides' into plants—an approach which, because of genetic adaptation in pests, will not provide the hoped-for 'final solution' to pest problems."—From a university press manuscript

Negative Characterizations and Condescending Expressions

2.15   Writers are urged to be sensitive to the classist connotations of words used to characterize members of a particular group, such as *deprived, disadvantaged, needy, underprivileged.* Children of a particular racial or ethnic group, for example, are not culturally deprived, educationally disadvantaged, or underprivileged, except perhaps in comparison to some implicit, putative norm. Writers should beware of assumptions regarding a relationship between race and socioeconomic status.

2.16   Designating countries as *undeveloped* or *underdeveloped* implies an evolutionary hierarchy of nations based on wealth, type of economy, and degree of industrialization. *Developing nations* is more widely accepted. The criteria for measuring development or lack of it should be clear if such terms are employed.

2.17   Gratuitous characterizations of individuals, such as *well-dressed, intelligent, articulate,* and *qualified*—e.g., *qualified minorities are encouraged to apply*—may be unacceptably patronizing in some contexts, as are positive stereotypes—the polite, hard-working Japanese person or the silver-tongued Irish person.

2.18   The condescending terms *boy* and *girl* to refer to adult persons of color should also be avoided.

Example 25: "An Eskimo boy, befriended by a Canadian cartographer, is sent down to Quebec to cure his TB, falls in love with a half-breed Indian girl, then reunites with her years later when they're serving in WW II England."—From a university film review

Example 26: "Unlike the other counties, [these counties] are burdened with large black populations."—From a university press manuscript

---

Artwork, Permissions

2.19   Graphic devices and clip art used by production and marketing staff can be generic and misleading—a cross motif on the dust jacket of a book about a non-Christian religion; a traditional Zuni design gracing chapter openings in a book about the Iroquois; an illustration of a geisha advertising a press's books on Japan. Art should be reviewed for appropriateness when selected to illustrate or market publications about race, ethnicity, nationality, or religion. Permission may be required to reproduce photographs of sacred objects and to use family and clan stories.

Specific Terms

aborigine/aboriginal. Capitalized if regarded as a proper name rather than a descriptive term. Widely used to refer to the aboriginal peoples of Australia, though some individuals prefer *Australian blacks*. When used to describe other indigenous peoples, these terms may carry the negative connotation—recorded without comment in *Webster's*—of "primitive in comparison with more advanced types."

African. Of or pertaining to the continent of Africa, its peoples, or its languages. Not a synonym for **black:** not all Africans are black.

African American. A currently preferred term referring to U.S. citizens of black African ancestry, though some people prefer **black.** *See also* **African, Afro-American, black American, colored/coloured, mulatto, Negro, Negroid.**

Afro-American. A term referring to U.S. citizens of black African ancestry. No longer widely used. **African Amer-**

ican and **black** are generally preferred in most contexts. *See also* **African, black American, colored/coloured, mulatto, Negro, Negroid.**

America/American. Guidelines disagree on the use of the term *American* to refer to a person from, or something pertaining to, the United States. The American Political Science Association's *Style Manual* advises writers to "use *United States, U.S., U.S. citizen,* or *citizen* in preference to *America(n)* when the country is meant; use *America(n)* for one or both continents only" (the name of the association itself illustrates the difficulty of changing the widespread equation of *American* with *U.S.*). The APSA manual particularly discourages as ethnocentric the use of *America* for the United States. The *McGraw-Hill Style Manual* advises against *American* in such formulations as *American policy* and *American economy,* where *U.S.* can be substituted; it accepts *American* for a United States citizen but recommends the use of *U.S. citizen* when it is necessary to distinguish from a citizen of a South American country or Canada. Immigrant groups that have settled in the United States are called *American:* e.g., *Chinese American, Irish American, Polish American.*

American Indian. Referring to indigenous peoples of North and South America and to their descendants, this term is favored by some over **Native American,** which is also accepted. Whenever possible, writers are encouraged to use the name of the specific people, e.g., *Cherokee* or *Crow,* rather than this umbrella term. References to skin color—*red, redskin*—are highly offensive, as are the many stereotypical terms that are still found in writing about American Indians—*brave, buck, chief* (used as a synonym for *Indian*), *half-breed, Indian maiden, massacre* (to refer to a successful American Indian raid or battle victory against white colonizers and invaders), *papoose, squaw, wampum, warpath.* The words *tepee* and *powwow* are accepted and used by some American Indians (indeed, pow-wows are an integral and important feature of modern life for many American Indian people), but the latter term should not be used in the incorrect sense of talks or negotiations. *See also* **Amerind/Amerindian, half-breed, Indian, native Indian.**

Amerind/Amerindian. These once-popular terms are no longer widely used in the United States. The term **American Indian** or **Native American** is preferable. *See also* **Indian.**

Anglo. Always capitalized. Although used in some parts of the United States to refer to any white person of non-Latin extraction, this term is etymologically incorrect and may be offensive: not all whites are of Anglo-Saxon descent; some individuals may resent an association with the English, e.g., a person of Irish heritage conscious of the history of England's oppression of Ireland. Refers more specifically and correctly to a person of English origin or descent or one whose language and culture are English. *See also* **Anglo-American, Caucasian, Caucasoid, English, white.**

Anglo-American. A U.S. inhabitant of English origin or descent or whose language and culture are English. Imprecise when used to refer to any white person of non-Latin extraction, regardless of national origin or ethnicity, who speaks English. *See also* **Anglo, Caucasian, Caucasoid, English, white.**

anglophone. The term used to designate English speakers in Canada. Not an ethnic identification. *See also* **francophone.**

Asian. Widely used to refer to peoples of or from Asia, even where a specific nationality would be more precise. In Canada writers are further urged to distinguish, when desirable, between *Southeast Asian* (from Burma, Thailand, Laos, Kampuchea, Vietnam, Malaysia, Indonesia, Singapore, Brunei, or the Philippines); *Central Asian* (including some of the countries of the former USSR and some autonomous regions of China, such as Inner Mongolia and Tibet); *East Asian* (from China, Japan, North or South Korea); and *South Asian* (from India, Pakistan, Bangladesh, Sri Lanka, Afghanistan, Nepal, or Bhutan). All these terms are acceptable—granted, what countries are included in the various regions of Asia varies according to context—but greater specificity is recommended (e.g., *Chinese, Japanese*) when possible. Asia is a large continent, and lumping all its inhabitants together under the term *Asian* is seldom usefully precise. *Asian* is not interchangeable with *Asian American*. Designation by skin color—*yellow*—is highly offensive. *See also* **Asiatic, Oriental.**

Asian American. The preferred generic term for Americans of Asian ancestry. Be specific when referring to particular Asian American groups (e.g., *Chinese American, Japanese American*). *See also* **Asian, Asiatic, Oriental.**

Asiatic. Asian. Often considered offensive, particularly when referring to people. Use **Asian** or be specific about national origin or ethnicity.

black. Widely accepted as a term referring to any person of black African ancestry, although **African American** is now favored by many U.S. citizens who are black, especially since some associate the term *black* with militancy or object to being identified by skin color rather than by origin and ancestry. Because the word is considered a generic or descriptive term, it is usually lowercased. Notwithstanding the unparallel usage *Black/white*, however, some writers strongly prefer the capitalized form on the analogy with other capitalized ethnic designations; the American Psychological Association recommends capitalization of both terms. Usage guidelines warn writers that the noun forms (*a black, blacks*) may be offensively reductionistic and recommend the adjectival form (*a black person, black people*). Although the designation *black* is widely (though not universally) accepted, other references to the skin color of a black person, such as *yellow* and *high yellow,* are derogatory. *See also* **African, Afro-American, black American, colored/coloured, mulatto, Negro, Negroid.**

black American. A U.S. citizen of black African ancestry. Acceptable but not as widely used as **African American** and **black**. *See also* **African, Afro-American, colored/coloured, mulatto, Negro, Negroid.**

British, Briton. Of or from the island of Great Britain, comprising England, Scotland, and Wales; a person from Great Britain. Not the same as **English;** inappropriate to describe a person from Northern Ireland. *See also* **United Kingdom.**

caste. Has a precise meaning in some societies. Writers must be sensitive to the accepted local terminology.

Half-caste is offensive; *outcaste* should be used with exceeding care.

Caucasian. Always capitalized. Based on an outmoded theory, the term refers to a "race" of people, including those of Latin extraction, rather than to a specific ethnic group or nationality. Although still used in many police departments and hospitals, the term is not recommended. Use **white** or specify ethnicity or nationality. *See also* **Anglo, Anglo-American, Caucasoid, English.**

Caucasoid. Derived from **Caucasian,** a term no longer generally accepted as a racial designation. The *-oid* ending carries a pejorative connotation. Not recommended. *See also* **Mongoloid, Negroid.**

Chicana/Chicano. A term widely used in the 1960s and 1970s to refer to U.S. residents of Mexican origin or ancestry and often carrying a connotation of political activism. Although still used on occasion, the term is considered offensive by some Mexican Americans; **Mexican American** is generally preferred. If the term is used, it should not be employed generically, i.e., to refer to any Spanish-speaking person regardless of origin or ancestry. *See also* **Hispanic, Hispanic American, Ibero-American, Latin American, Latina/Latino, Spanish.**

Chinaman. A man of Chinese ancestry. Highly pejorative.

Chinatown. A term referring to the Chinese quarter of a city. Should not be used as an umbrella term for all Asian American communities.

Chinese. Of or pertaining to China, its peoples, or its languages. Not all Chinese are Han Chinese; there are many ethnic groups (for example, Mongol). *Chinese* is not interchangeable with *Chinese American.*

colored/coloured. Black. In some societies, including the United States, the word is derogatory and should not be used except when it is part of a formal name (e.g., the National Association for the Advancement of Colored People) or when it occurs in a historical document. In South Africa, *coloured* refers to persons of mixed black African and other ancestry, and the term may be used in discussions of ethnicities in South African society. *See also* **African, Afro-American, African American, black, black American, Creole, mulatto, Negro, Negroid, people of color, person of mixed ancestry.**

coolie. An unskilled laborer or porter. Pejorative. Use *laborer, worker,* or *porter.*

Cosa Nostra. A Sicilian organization. Discriminatory against Italians unless used in the precise, historically correct sense. Use *organized crime. See also* **Mafia.**

Creole. A person of European descent born especially in the West Indies or Spanish America; a white person descended from early French or Spanish settlers of the U.S. Gulf states and preserving their speech or culture; a person of mixed French or Spanish and black African descent speaking a dialect of French or Spanish. *See also* **person of mixed ancestry, half-breed, mulatto, colored/coloured, Métis.**

developing country/nation. *See* **newly industrializing country (NIC).**

emerging country/nation. *See* **newly industrializing country (NIC).**

English. Of or from England. Should be distinguished from **British.** *See also* **United Kingdom.**

Eskimo. Of or pertaining to a group of peoples of northern Canada, Greenland, Alaska, and eastern Siberia. Although *Eskimo* is still widely used, it is a pejorative term that was adopted by Europeans (it means, roughly, "eaters of raw meat"). The term **Inuk** (plural, **Inuit**) is preferred by Arctic and Canadian peoples and is the recommended alternative; also spelled with two *n*'s: *Innuk, Innuit.*

Euro-American. An accepted term, still in use, especially in archeology and history, but increasingly replaced by **European American.**

Eurasian. Designates a person of mixed European and Asian ancestry; considered derogatory by many individuals. *See* **person of mixed ancestry.**

European American. An American of European ancestry. The term has come into favor, along with **Anglo-American,** as a way of avoiding the suggestion that the unqualified term *American* means "white" and is the norm from which "hyphenated Americans" depart. *See also* **Euro-American.**

Far East. Eurocentric. *East Asia* is now preferred.

francophone. The term used to designate French speakers in Canada. Not an ethnic identification. *See also* **anglophone.**

gentile. In general, anyone who is not a Jew; more specifically, a Christian. To Mormons, however, the term means one who is not Mormon.

ghetto. A quarter of a city in which members of an ethnic or religious group live, especially because of social, legal, or economic pressure. Because the word is loaded with negative connotations—poverty, crime, dilapidation, persecution—more neutral terms, such as *community, neighborhood,* and *quarter,* are often preferable. The expression *ghetto blaster* for a portable stereo (or, more colloquially, a "boom box") is offensive as a stereotype of African American culture.

half-breed. A derogatory term sometimes used to refer to a person of mixed white and American Indian or other mixed ancestry. The terms *half-blood* and *mixed-blood* are acceptable for a person of mixed American Indian and other ancestry. *See also* **colored/coloured** (in the South African context), **Eurasian, Métis, person of mixed ancestry.**

heathen. A person who does not acknowledge the God of the Christian scriptures. Also carrying the pejorative connotation of "uncivilized or irreligious," the term is offensive when used to characterize indigenous peoples or those who are not Christian. It is preferable to specify the religion or belief system, e.g., *animism, Buddhism, Hinduism, traditional religion, polytheism. See also* **pagan.**

Hispanic. As an adjective, means Spanish-speaking or, more specifically, descended from Spanish-speaking people from Mexico, Central or South America, or the Caribbean. Some usage guidelines recommend not using the term in its noun forms (*a Hispanic, Hispanics*), whereas other authorities accept this usage but recommend greater specificity when possible. *See also* **Chicana/Chicano, Hispanic American, Ibero-American, Latin American, Latina/Latino, Mexican American, Spanish.**

Hispanic American. Often used to refer to all U.S. residents who speak Spanish as a first language and/or, in place of *Latin American,* to refer to those who are one or two generations removed from Spanish-speaking people from Mexico, Central or South America, or the Caribbean. An accepted term, though some object to it because it emphasizes a shared European heritage rather than various cultural heritages of the Western Hemisphere, because not all Spanish-speaking peoples in the Western Hemisphere are of Spanish descent, and because the term is sometimes used to include individuals who do not speak Spanish, e.g., French- and Portuguese-speaking people of South American or Caribbean ancestry. **Mexican American** and **Latin American** are sometimes preferred, and greater specificity is recommended in the latter category when possible—e.g., *Central American, South American, Brazilian. See also* **Chicana/Chicano, Hispanic, Ibero-American, Latina/Latino, Spanish.**

Ibero-American. An alternative to **Hispanic American.** Acceptable, but subject to the same objections as the latter term and not widely used. *See also* **Chicana/Chicano, Hispanic, Latin American, Latina/Latino, Mexican American, Spanish.**

illegal alien. A term referring to a person in the United States without a visa. **Undocumented resident** or **undocumented worker** is generally preferred as less pejorative. *See also* **wetback.**

Indian. An individual from, or pertaining to, India; incorrect when applied to a person from a South Asian country other than India. In the United States, the preferred terms for indigenous peoples of North America and their descendants are **American Indian** and **Native American;** in Canada, *Indians* is sometimes used to designate aboriginal Canadians who are not Aleut or **Inuk;** these latter terms, along with **native Indian, native peoples,** and the names of specific nations or peoples are preferred as more precise. Note, however, that some American Indians do refer to themselves simply as *Indian* or *Indian people;* writers may choose to use the term if it is preferred and may also judiciously employ ıt in the context of pre-twentieth-century U.S. history, where the twentieth-century terms might seem anachronistic.

Inuk (sing.)**/Inuit** (pl.) **(Innuk/Innuit).** Of or pertaining to a group of peoples of northern Canada, Greenland, Alaska, and eastern Siberia. Preferred by Arctic and Canadian peoples to the widely used term **Eskimo.** The single-consonant spellings are used in the Arctic volume of the Smithsonian's new edition of the authoritative *Handbook of North American Indians,* but the double-consonant forms are also recognized.

Islam. The religious faith of Muslims, including belief in Allah as the sole deity and in **Muhammad** as his prophet. *Islamic* and **Muslim** are both accepted adjective forms.

Israeli. A citizen of Israel. Not interchangeable with **Jew:** not all Israelis are Jews, and not all Jews are citizens of Israel. The word *Israeli* came into being in 1948 and should not be used to refer to individuals before that date.

issei. A first-generation Japanese American, one who has immigrated to the United States. *See also* **nisei.**

Japanese. Of or pertaining to Japan, its peoples, or its languages. Not interchangeable with *Japanese American.*

Jew. A person whose religion or cultural heritage is Jewish. Some people find the noun form objectionable (*a Jew, Jews*) and recommend the adjectival inflection (*a Jewish person, Jewish people*). Describes an ethnicity, not a race: of Jewish background, not Jewish race. *See also* **Israeli.**

landed immigrant. The term formerly applied to a legal resident of Canada who had not taken Canadian citizenship. The current preferred term is *permanent resident.*

Latin American. Refers to citizens of Latin American countries. Also, the most widely used term to refer to U.S. residents who are Spanish-speaking and/or are of Mexican, Central American, South American, or Caribbean ancestry. Although generally preferred to *Hispanic American,* some object to the term because not all persons referred to as Latin American speak a Latin-based language, because the term glosses over national differences, and because it usually does not include French speakers. Greater specificity is recommended—e.g., *Central American, South American, Brazilian. See also* **Chicana/Chicano, Hispanic, Hispanic American, Ibero-American, Latina/Latino, Mexican American, Spanish.**

Latina/Latino. As an adjective, means Spanish-speaking or, more specifically, descended from Spanish-speaking people from Mexico, Central or South America, or the Caribbean. Although preferred by some groups to *Hispanic,* the terms are not always interchangeable, since *Latina/Latino* is sometimes understood to refer only to those of Latin American ancestry and to exclude Mexican Americans. Some usage guidelines recommend not using the term in its noun forms (*a Latina, Latinas*), whereas other authorities accept this usage but recommend greater specificity. *See also* **Chicana/Chicano, Hispanic, Hispanic American, Ibero-American, Latin American, Mexican American, Spanish.**

Mafia. Organized independent groups of brigands that arose in Sicily probably in the nineteenth century. Following a feudal tradition, the Mafia disdained legal authorities, sought justice through direct action (such as the vendetta), and observed a rigid code of secrecy, traditions that enabled some *Mafiosi* to rise in organized crime after coming to the United States as Italian immigrants. Discriminatory against Italian Americans unless used in the correct historical sense; not interchangeable with *organized crime,* a more generic term. *See also* **Cosa Nostra.**

Métis. The old French term *métis,* meaning "mixed," applied to persons of dual white and native Indian ancestry since the initial settlement of Canada by Europeans. The capitalized term refers to those who identify themselves as an ethnic group with a distinct sociocultural heritage. *See also* **half-breed, person of mixed ancestry.**

Mexican American. The preferred term to refer to U.S. residents of Mexican origin or ancestry. *See also* **Chicana/Chicano, Hispanic, Hispanic American, Ibero-American, Latin American, Latina/Latino, Spanish.**

Mohammed. *See* **Muhammad.**

Mongoloid. Derived from Mongolian, the term is no longer used, and the *-oid* suffix has a pejorative connotation. *See also* **Caucasoid, Negroid.**

Mormon. A member of the Church of Jesus Christ of Latter-day Saints. The religious institution is more properly designated by this name, although it is sometimes informally called the Mormon Church.

Moslem. An older spelling. Use **Muslim.**

Muhammad. Arab prophet. Preferred to *Mohammed.*

Muhammadan. Old-fashioned and offensive term for **Muslim.**

mulatto. From the Spanish word *mulo,* "mule," the term refers to a person of mixed white and African American ancestry. It is often considered offensive, and the term **person of mixed ancestry** is preferred. *See also* **colored/coloured.**

Muslim. Preferred to *Moslem* and *Muhammadan* to refer to a person whose religion is Islam or to designate something of or pertaining to Islam. Note that the term is not interchangeable with *Arab* or *Arabian:* not all Muslims are Arab, and not all Arabs are Muslim.

native. Describes an indigenous inhabitant. The capitalized noun *Native,* without modifiers, is commonly used in both Canada and Alaska as an umbrella term for Indians, Inuit, and Aleuts. Writers should, however, be aware of the lingering pejorative connotation, in some contexts, of "one inhabiting a territorial area at the time it is discovered by or becomes familiar to a foreigner; one having a less complex civilization."

native American. One born in the United States, i.e., a native-born citizen.

Native American. Refers to indigenous North American peoples and their descendants. In disfavor with some American Indians because the U.S. government now includes Alaskan Natives (Indians, Inuit, and Aleuts of Alaska), Samoans, and Native Hawaiians under this term. **American Indian** is now the generally preferred term, although some native peoples still strongly favor the former, once more popular, term. Whenever possible, writers are encouraged to use the name of the specific peoples rather than either umbrella term. *See also* **Amerind/Amerindian, Indian, native Indian.**

native Indian. A Canadian term referring to indigenous peoples of Canada, excluding the **Inuit;** equivalent to the U.S. terms **American Indian** and **Native American.** As in writing about American Indians, greater specificity is recommended. *See also* **native.**

native peoples. Designates indigenous peoples. In Canada, the preferred comprehensive term referring to the eight **Inuit** nations, the numerous nations loosely called **native Indian,** and the **Métis.**

Near East. Eurocentric. *Middle East* is now preferred.

Negro. Acceptable in the proper historical context but otherwise dated. **African American** and **black** are generally preferred in most contexts. The feminine-inflected form, *Negress,* is antiquated and pejorative. *See also* **African, Afro-American, black American, colored/coloured, mulatto, Negroid.**

Negroid. Derived from **Negro,** a term no longer in general use. The *-oid* ending carries a pejorative connotation. Not recommended. *See also* **Caucasoid, Mongoloid.**

new Canadian. A term, now out of fashion, referring to an immigrant who has assumed Canadian citizenship.

newly industrializing (*or* newly industrialized)

country (NIC). A country that has begun to show rapid industrial development. When specifically applicable, this term is preferred to *developing* or *emerging country* or *nation,* terms which imply an evolutionary hierarchy of countries and connote "backwardness" as well as "progress." *See also* **third world, etc.**

New World/Old World. Eurocentric.

nisei. A second-generation Japanese American, and therefore not an immigrant. *See also* **issei.**

nonwhite. Objectionable in some contexts because it makes white the standard by which individuals are classified (*white/nonwhite*). Some people prefer the opposition *white people/people of color.* Greater specificity is preferred whenever possible. *See also* **visible minorities.**

Okie. A migrant agricultural worker, especially one from Oklahoma in the 1930s. Pejorative.

Orient/Oriental. The East, Eastern, Easterner, as opposed to Occident/Occidental, which is now usually replaced with West/Westerner. All these terms are imprecise; *Orient* and *Occident* are old-fashioned as well, although the former still lingers in some academic fields—*Oriental studies, orientalist*—especially in Europe. The adjectival form is objectionable; the noun forms *Oriental* and *Orientals,* used to describe people, are highly offensive to some individuals. *Asian* or a more specific term is preferred.

pagan. A follower of a polytheistic religion. Also carrying the pejorative connotation of "irreligious and hedonistic," the term is offensive when used to characterize indigenous peoples or those who are not Christian. It is preferable to specify the religion or belief system, e.g., *animism, Buddhism, Hinduism, traditional religion, polytheism.* Some followers of new religions, however, use *pagan* in a positive sense to describe their religious beliefs and to distinguish themselves from Christian traditions. *See also* **heathen.**

people of color. Preferred to **nonwhite,** which suggests that white is the standard. *See also* **visible minorities.**

people/peoples. Preferred to **tribe** as a term to identify distinct indigenous or ethnic groups—e.g., *the Pueblo peoples.*

person of mixed ancestry. The term preferred over the pejorative expressions **Eurasian, half-breed,** and **mulatto.** *See also* **colored/coloured** (in the South African context), **Métis.**

project. A shortened form for *public housing project.* Usually associated with U.S. minorities, both terms, like **ghetto,** have come to carry negative connotations—poverty, crime, dilapidation. The expressions *public housing development* and *subsidized housing* are preferable.

Quran. The scriptures of Islam. Preferred to *Koran.*

refugee. One who has fled a foreign country or power to escape danger or persecution. Not all immigrants are refugees.

Russian. An individual from, or pertaining to, Russia. Not interchangeable with **Soviet.**

Scottish, Scots, Scotch. *Scots* refers to the people of Scotland, *Scottish* is the adjectival form, and *Scotch* is reserved for certain products or objects (such as whisky).

Soviet. An individual from, or pertaining to, the former USSR. Not interchangeable with **Russian.**

Spanish. As a noun, refers to the language; as an adjective, means an individual from, or pertaining to, Spain. Not interchangeable with *Mexican, Latina/Latino,* or *Hispanic.*

third world, developing, emerging, nonindustrialized, underdeveloped, undeveloped. Because these terms basically mean not rich, industrialized, or highly technological, and contain an implicit comparison with the countries that are, each in turn comes to have derogatory meanings, absorbed through use. The terms lump together many very different countries. Often one can be usefully precise: Southeast Asian countries whose GNP is less than $X or less than X percent of whose GNP is related to manufacturing. In addition to economic denotations, *third world* has a political one, namely, neutral or not aligned with either the United States or the former USSR and their allies—a meaning now of dubious applicability. In the United States *third world* also refers to minority groups taken as a whole. More specific terms are often preferable to this imprecise, sweeping designation, with its connotation of a hierarchy of nations or ethnicities.

tribe/tribal. May apply to the organization of some American Indian groups, and some accept these terms; but not all American Indians have "tribal" organization. As a term identifying a distinct indigenous group, whether of Native Americans or Africans, *tribe* dates from the nineteenth century and in some contexts may carry negative connotations of "primitive" or "backward."

Often preferable are **nation** or **people** (e.g., *the Iroquois nation*, referring to the confederacy of *Iroquois peoples*) or a specific designation (e.g., *the Blackfoot, the Zulu*). The adjectival form *tribal* may carry the same negative connotations—as in *tribal warfare* to describe conflicts between American Indian or African peoples but not comparable ethnic conflicts in Europe—and may fail to differentiate religious, cultural, economic, and political bases of conflict between peoples.

undocumented resident/undocumented worker. The preferred term to designate a person in the United States without a visa. *See also* **illegal alien, wetback.**

United Kingdom. Officially, the United Kingdom of Great Britain and Northern Ireland, comprising England, Scotland, and Wales on the island of Great Britain, and Northern Ireland on the island of Ireland. A person from Northern Ireland is a U.K. citizen but should not be referred to as **British** or **English.**

visible minorities. This phrase is used in Canada to refer to citizens who are **blacks, native peoples, Asians,** and others not of European descent. The term is preferable to **nonwhite,** which suggests that white is the standard, but not to a more precise term. As an expression meaning "not of European descent," it should be used with caution: a European American is a member of a visible minority in Japan.

WASP. White Anglo-Saxon Protestant, a term of limited application. Not interchangeable with **white** or **Anglo:** not all white people are English-speaking or of English ancestry; nor are they, or all Anglo people, necessarily Protestant.

West/East. Broad, imprecise terms that lend themselves to stereotyping (as do *Occidental/Oriental*). To talk about the East as exotic, mysterious, and inscrutable is as inappropriate as to characterize the West as crass, materialistic, immoral, and energetic. Nonetheless, scholars in religious studies, for example, still write about "the wisdom of the East" as though Asians had arcane knowledge.

wetback. A derogatory term often referring to a Mexican person in the United States without a visa. **Undocumented resident** or **undocumented worker** is preferred. *See also* **illegal alien.**

white. The generally accepted term to refer to any white person of non-Latin extraction. In many contexts, *white* includes people of Latin descent as well and may also refer to individuals of European descent at second remove—for example, people of European stock born in Brazil who went to Hawaii in the nineteenth century; a Spaniard in the Philippines. The American Psychological Association recommends capitalization of the terms *black* and *white,* although many other style manuals, including the *Chicago Manual of Style,* favor lowercasing them. *See also* **Anglo, Anglo-American, Caucasian, Caucasoid, English.**

3

Disabilities and Medical Conditions

Disability and Handicap

3.1   A *disability* is a medically defined condition, or *impairment,* that substantially limits one or more of a person's major life activities, such as performing manual tasks, walking, seeing, hearing, speaking, breathing, working, and learning. According to the federal definition, a person also has a disability if he or she has a history of such a condition but no longer experiences it (for example, some heart problems) or is perceived to have such a condition (for example, a facial disfigurement). Not all disabilities are visible or physical.

3.2   Usage guidelines for writing about people with disabilities usually distinguish between the terms *disability* and *handicap*. Whereas a disability is a physical, mental, or psychological impairment, a *handicap* is an environmental or attitudinal barrier to the independence of disabled people. Stairs and narrow doorways are handicaps to a person who uses a wheelchair; an employer's refusal to provide adaptive telephone equipment is a handicap to a worker with impaired hearing. Laws and regulations, however, often employ the term *handicap* as a synonym for *disability*.

3.3   Businesses and government offices sometimes describe their facilities as *handicap accessible* (or just *accessible*) when in fact the meaning is simply "accessible to wheelchair users." This restricted use of the term is misleading. Properly used, *accessible* includes individuals with visual, hearing, and other impairments as well; it can also pertain to older persons and to children.

Able-Bodied, Normal, Nondisabled

3.4   All individuals have, and make adaptations to, different degrees of ability: an infant or very young child depends on adults; a person with arthritis may use a cane; a person with astigmatism may wear glasses. The term *able-bodied* obscures this continuum of ability and may perpetuate an invidious distinction between persons so designated and those with disabilities. It should be used with caution.

3.5   The term *normal* may legitimately refer to a statistical norm for human ability ("Normal vision is 20/20") but should usually be avoided in other contexts as similarly invidious.

> **Example 27:** "She also has iodine deficiency,
> . . . which might explain why she has had
> only one completely normal child out of
> seven. Four died at or near birth; of three sur-
> viving sons one is a cretin, one is normal ex-
> cept that he is quite deaf and therefore also
> dumb, and one is normal. The cretin is most
> pathetic. . . . Fortunately he never cries."
> —From a university press manuscript

3.6   Some writers deliberately challenge "normalism"—the
assumption that the norm for human abilities is the fully
independent young adult with optimal physical and mental prowess—by using such terms as *temporarily able-bodied*
and *nondisabled*. These terms seem unnecessarily polem-
ical and circumlocutory; outside consciously political contexts they have not gained much currency and are not
recommended.

Alternative Terms

3.7   *Disabled* is the most widely accepted adjective. Many alternatives have been proposed, among them *physically* (or
mentally) *different, differently abled, physically challenged, excep-
tional,* and *special* or *special needs* (as in *special needs children*).
Some writers prefer these terms as less judgmental than
disabled, and such alternatives may be appropriate in some
contexts, particularly if a writer's purpose is to challenge

readers' preconceptions. In other contexts the expressions may seem euphemistic, suggesting, perhaps, that disabled people belong to a different or uncommonly rare species or that having a disability is an exciting adventure. In still other contexts the terms are insufficiently precise. An acquisitions librarian at Gallaudet University, an educational institution for people with hearing impairments, wrote a university press to complain that she was unable to ascertain from its titles whether certain publications treated the subject of deafness: "The current trend toward some vagueness in describing materials makes selecting and purchasing a difficult process. No one wants to 'label' anyone, but it is necessary to know what condition is being discussed."

3.8 We recommend that writers employ direct, precise language rather than euphemisms in describing disabilities, taking care, however, to avoid the kinds of disparaging labels and characterizations described below.

Disparaging Labels and Characterizations

3.9 Converting adjectival forms into nouns reduces individuals to conditions or attaches disparaging labels to groups, as in the expressions *an amputee, an arthritic, a cripple, an epileptic, the deaf, paraplegics,* and especially *the handicapped* (from *hand in cap,* which actually derives from a game of chance but is mistakenly associated with beggary). Some individuals object as well to *the disabled;* others accept it as a useful self-identifier similar to such words as *blacks* or *gays* (though some object to these words as well).

3.10   Guidelines for writing about people with disabilities en-
            courage writers to seek phrasing that emphasizes individ-
            uality: a person *with* (or *living with*) *arthritis, who has a
            mobility impairment, who is affected by epilepsy;* people *who
            are deaf* or *who experience paraplegia.* These phrasings may
            be replaced or alternated with nonderogatory adjectives—
            a deaf person, disabled people. But guidelines stress the de-
            sirability of "getting the person before the disability"
            whenever possible.

3.11   The "language of disease" can incorrectly suggest that a
            disabled person is in ill health or is receiving medical
            treatment—*a multiple sclerosis case, a mental patient.* These
            phrases are appropriate only if the person has a disease
            that requires a physician's care. In other contexts, *condi-
            tion* is more precise than *disease.*

3.12   The "language of victimization," characterizing a disabled
            person as a victim, may reinforce negative stereotypes of
            passivity and helplessness: *a victim of MS,* a person *stricken
            with polio, suffering from epilepsy, afflicted with mental illness,
            confined to a wheelchair* or *wheelchair-bound.* Adjectives such
            as *poor* and *unfortunate* have a similar effect and are pa-
            tronizing, as are, conversely, such epithets as *heroic* and
            courageous.

3.13   Such terms as *crippled, deficient, defective, deformed, invalid,
            lame, maimed, unfit,* and *withered* likewise have negative
            connotations in their adjectival and especially in their
            noun forms (*a defective, the lame, the unfit*).

3.14 Instead of emphasizing limitations, writers can stress survival and adaptive abilities, saying, for example, *a polio survivor, a wheelchair user* or *person who uses a wheelchair, who walks with crutches,* or *who is partially sighted.*

3.15 Disabilities serve as metaphors in some stock phrases. Such expressions as *deaf to our wishes* or *blind to the truth* are innocent in some contexts but may be inappropriate or unintentionally offensive in others. Writers should keep in mind that many people with disabilities are readers of university press books.

Specific Terms

Writers can generally both avoid offense and remain faithful to their craft by being precise and specific: *a person with such-and-such a disability* rather than *a disabled person.* The following terms may be of assistance.

AIDS. Acquired Immune Deficiency Syndrome. A severe immunological disorder caused by the retrovirus **HIV** and resulting in increased susceptibility to opportunistic infections and certain rare cancers. A person does not die from AIDS but from complications of AIDS. AIDS is a sexually transmitted disease affecting individuals of all cultures, economic and social classes, sexes, and sexual orientations; it is not "a gay disease."

blindness. Total loss of vision. The adjective *blind* does not correctly describe a *partially sighted* person, that is, a person with a partial loss of vision. Partially sighted persons are sometimes referred to as *visually impaired* or *sight-impaired*.

cerebral palsy. A general term for a group of disabling conditions resulting from central nervous system damage. The adjectival form *cerebral palsied* is no longer accepted. *See also* **Spasticity.**

cleft lip and palate. A person with a *cleft lip* has a visible congenital anomaly affecting facial appearance but usually not speech; the term *harelip* is no longer considered acceptable. A *cleft palate* is an anomaly affecting the internal structure of the mouth that is usually not visible but that is often associated with speech difficulties.

communicative disorder. A general term for speech, hearing, and learning disabilities that affect a person's ability to communicate.

congenital disability. A disability that has existed since birth. This term is preferable to *birth defect,* which has a strongly negative connotation.

deafness. Total loss of hearing. *Hearing impaired* refers to a person with a *partial hearing loss.* The set expressions *deaf and dumb* and *deaf-mute,* suggesting that all deaf or hearing-impaired persons are incapable of speech, are inaccurate and offensive. (In a speech at Gallaudet University, the university's president once referred to the hearing members of the audience as *Sign-impaired.*)

developmental disability. Any mental and/or physical disability manifested before adulthood that may continue indefinitely, resulting in substantial limitation of life activities. The adjectival form is *developmentally disabled.* The term includes individuals with mental retardation, cerebral palsy, spina bifida, autism, and sensory impairments.

Down syndrome (*or* **Down's syndrome).** A form of mental retardation caused by improper chromosomal division during gestation. Either medical term is preferable to *mongolism* and *mongoloid,* which are considered disparaging. Although several standard dictionaries, including *Webster's New World,* 3d ed., and *Merriam-Webster's Collegiate Dictionary,* 10th ed., list the form *Down's* first, others, such as *American Heritage Dictionary,* 3d ed., prefer *Down*— a choice endorsed by two forthcoming references for medical editors, the twenty-eighth edition of *Dorland's Medical Dictionary* and the sixth edition of the *CBE Style Manual (Scientific Style and Format),* and also strongly recommended by the Down Syndrome Society.

dwarfism. A general term covering a large number of medical conditions resulting in severe short stature, sometimes accompanied by disproportionate body development. Medical literature often refers to an affected individual as a *dwarf,* and this term is acceptable in a context clearly describing a person's medical condition, although a more precise term, such as *person with achondroplasia,* is preferable if the specific condition is known. However, the pejorative connotations of the word *dwarf* make it objectionable to many individuals, who recommend *little person* (sometimes capitalized), *person of short stature,* or *short-statured person*—acceptable alternatives provided the meaning is clear in context. The term *midget,* once used to describe a little person with proportionate body growth, is now considered derogatory. Writers should be sensitive to metaphorical uses of any of these terms that invoke negative connotations (e.g., *a dwarf among men, a mental midget*).

epilepsy. A seizure disorder marked by disturbed electrical rhythms of the central nervous system. Manifestations of epilepsy are termed *seizures,* not *fits.*

HIV. Human immunodeficiency virus (*HIV virus* is redundant), the virus believed to lead to **AIDS.**

mental illness/mental disorder. Loss of the social and/or vocational skills necessary to function independently. *Mental disorder* is the more comprehensive term and may be used to describe any of the recognized forms of mental illness or several emotional disorders. Terms such as *mentally deranged, mentally unbalanced, mentally diseased, insane, deviant, demented,* and *crazy* are not appropriate; terms such as *neurotic, psychopathic,* and *schizophrenic* should be reserved for technical and medical writing.

mental retardation. A condition in which a person has significantly below-average general intellectual functioning. Labels such as *feebleminded, idiot, imbecile, mentally defective, mentally deficient, moron,* and *retard* are considered offensive.

Siamese twins. *Conjoined twins* is the preferred term.

spasticity. A condition characterized by sudden, abnormal involuntary muscle spasms. Muscles are spastic; to call a person with spasticity *a spastic* is considered offensive.

specific learning disability. A disorder in the ability to learn effectively in an average educational environment. As currently used, the term does not include visual, hearing, or motor impairments, mental retardation, or emotional disturbance, although these conditions may also affect learning ability. The adjective *specific* is preferred because it indicates that the disability affects only certain learning processes.

speech impairment. A condition characterized by limited or difficult speech patterns. The terms *dumb* and *mute* are considered disparaging, and words such as *stutter,* *stammer,* and *lisp* carry emotional connotations that are often inappropriate or misleading.

4

Sexual Orientation

4.1   Language designating same-sex and bisexual orientation
is undergoing rapid change. There is little agreement
concerning clear, acceptable, nonderogatory terms.

*Sexual Preference, Sexual Orientation, and
Sexual Status*

4.2   Most people do not consider their sexuality a matter of
choice. *Sexual preference* implies otherwise and is often in-
equitably applied only to those with a same-sex or bisexual
orientation. *Sexual orientation,* which can apply to a heterosexual, homosexual, or bisexual person, is preferable. *Sexual status,* a term that has been used by individuals in public
debate over the participation of gay men and lesbians in
the military services, is unacceptably vague.

Gay, Lesbian, Homosexual, Queer, Same-Sex

4.3   Both the noun and the adjectival forms of *gay* are now
strongly gender-marked as masculine in most contexts: *a*

gay (man), gays, gay men. Women with a same-sex orientation generally prefer *lesbian* (note that because *lesbian* means "homosexual woman," the expression *lesbian woman* is redundant). Hence the common pairing in both noun and adjectival uses is *gay and lesbian* or vice versa: *gay men and lesbians, lesbians and gays, lesbian and gay issues.* Even though *gays* and *gay* sometimes still serve as the common-gender noun and adjectival forms designating both women and men, especially when discussed together (*gays celebrate, gay publications, gay pride*), these usages are ambiguous and also objectionable because they subsume women under a gender-marked masculine term.

4.4   *Gay* is now a widely accepted term to describe men with a same-sex orientation. In writing about contemporary subjects many authors prefer the word to *homosexual* because it avoids the negative connotations of the latter term and because it conveys not just sexual orientation but also the cultural and social aspects of homosexuality.

4.5   Some style manuals advise restricting *gay* to adjectival uses (*a gay man/gay men,* not *a gay/gays*). Although many gay and lesbian publications do not strictly follow this recommendation, writers should be aware that, like other names of social groups derived from adjectives, the noun form may be offensively reductionistic ("There were two gays on the panel"; cf. "There were two blacks on the panel"). Accordingly, the adjectival use is preferable, and the noun form should be employed, if at all, with caution.

4.6   Although many writers now avoid *homosexual* because of negative connotations of pathology or criminal behavior, some individuals with a same-sex orientation still accept it as a term referring to either a woman or a man and may prefer *homosexual man/homosexual woman* because of the still-ambiguous gender marking of *gay*. Others use the terms *gay* and *homosexual* interchangeably. *Homosexual* is preferable in pre–World War II contexts and in references to some traditional or non-Western cultures, where *gay* would seem anachronistic or discordant. A writer may also choose this term to refer to individuals or groups who strongly prefer it.

4.7   Long avoided as pejorative, *queer* has recently made a comeback among some lesbians and gays as a term referring to both women and men (e.g., *the Queer Nation*); other normally derogatory terms, such as *dyke, faggot,* and *queen,* are also sometimes used in a positive sense. Still, many continue to find these terms objectionable. Like other hate words defiantly revalued by the very individuals against whom they have been directed (cf. *nigger, hussy*), these terms are offensive if employed by an outsider and are usually employed in gay and lesbian publications to refer only to specific groups that prefer them.

4.8   Some writers employ the adjective *same-sex* interchangeably with *gay* or *lesbian* to describe sexual orientation or relationship.

Relationships

4.9   Many individuals prefer *lover* to describe the relationship of a gay or lesbian couple. But whether the word is used to refer to a heterosexual or a homosexual bond, it may place an undesired emphasis on the sexual and intimate aspects of the relationship to the exclusion of other aspects.

4.10 *Partner, domestic partner,* or *life partner* is also used for both homosexual and heterosexual unions but carries the connotation of a business relationship, which may be unsuitable in some contexts.

4.11 *Significant other,* also applying to both same-sex and heterosexual unions, appears to be passing out of favor. Although it still appears in some contexts ("Employees and their significant others are cordially invited to the festivities"), it often seems dated or facetious.

4.12 *Companion, domestic companion,* or *longtime companion,* which also apply to a heterosexual or same-sex union, are widely recognized and are gaining in favor. The term *companion* has been adopted by the *Wall Street Journal* and is recommended by Wayne Dynes, editor of *Encyclopedia of Homosexuality.*

Heterosexism

4.13 Besides choosing appropriate designations for sexual orientation, sensitive writers seek to avoid terms and statements implying or assuming that heterosexuality is the norm for sexual attraction (and hence homosexual attraction "deviant") and that all domestic arrangements are founded on a heterosexual union of two people:

> When a mother is employed, her husband may discover that his share of the childcare has increased.

> Some gays in long-term relationships establish relational networks beyond the individual couple that can approach the nature of real family ties.

4.14   Instead of *husband, wife,* or *spouse,* writers are encouraged to use the more inclusive terms listed above to refer to relationships where appropriate; instead of *marriage,* they may employ terms such as *committed relationship* or *primary relationship;* and for *marriage counseling,* they may substitute *couples therapy* or *relationship counseling.*

4.15   Writers should likewise avoid phrasing that marginalizes individuals with a same-sex orientation. The statement

> AIDS education must extend beyond the gay male population to the general population

suggests that gay men are not part of the "general" (heterosexual?) population, a bias more obvious to some readers when one substitutes, say, "black" for "gay male." Writers should also beware statements that implicitly associate lesbians or gay men with criminal or pathological behavior:

> Psychologists need training in working with special populations such as lesbians, drug abusers, and alcoholics.

5

Age

5.1   Although many style manuals caution against ageism—bias against individuals on the basis of age—few offer specific guidelines for usage. Writers are enjoined to avoid gratuitous references to age and to eschew negative or sentimental stereotypes. A few terms referring to age warrant comment here.

Young Persons

5.2   According to most guidelines, *boy* and *girl* apply to individuals up to about the age of thirteen or fourteen.

5.3   *Youth* may apply to a person of either sex between the ages of thirteen and nineteen, or a writer may use the terms preferred by many individuals in this age group: *young person, young man,* or *young woman.*

5.4   Although *teenager* and *adolescent* are also used to describe a person between these ages, these terms may carry un-

wanted connotations because of their frequent occur-
rence in phrases referring to social and behavioral problems among young people (e.g., *teenage pregnancy, teenage
driver, adolescent behavior*) that contribute to age stereotyping. *Juvenile,* which properly describes any minor person
but is popularly applied to adolescents, likewise may seem
derogatory because of its associations (*juvenile delinquency,
juvenile opinions*).

5.5   *Young adult* is preferable for individuals in their late teens,
and, since it also applies to individuals in their twenties,
it avoids the age segregation of *teenager* and like terms.

Older Persons

5.6   The term *older person* is now generally preferred to *elder*
and *elderly person* in referring to an individual past what
is commonly recognized as middle age, or the period of
life from about forty to sixty.

5.6   *Elders* may, of course, be used in contexts invoking the
positive connotations of the term (e.g., "The matter was
submitted to the community elders for decision").

5.7   Although *senior* and *senior citizen* are also accepted, their
greater age specificity (they usually mean "sixty-five or
older") makes them unsuitable in some contexts.

5.8   *Senility* is a medical condition that affects only a small percentage of older people, and Alzheimer's disease occasionally affects younger people as well. Writers are urged to avoid casual comments assuming an inevitable link between aging and forgetfulness or senility (e.g., "she's getting forgetful in her old age," "he must be getting senile").

Select Bibliography

American Association of Retired Persons. 1984. *Truth about Aging: Guidelines for Accurate Communication*. Washington, DC. [A 36-page pamphlet focusing more on underrepresentation, misrepresentation, and stereotypes of older persons than on specific usages. Available from AARP, 1909 K Street N.W., Washington, DC 20049.]

American Psychological Association. 1994. "Guidelines to Reduce Bias in Language." In *Publications Manual of the American Psychological Association*, 4th ed., pp. 46–60. Washington, DC. [A readily available and widely used style manual for social scientists containing recently updated guidelines for writing about gender, sexual orientation, race and ethnicity, disability, and age.]

Frank, Francine Wattman, and Paula A. Treichler, eds. 1989. *Language, Gender, and Professional Writing: Theoretical Approaches and Guidelines for Nonsexist Usage*. New York: Modern Language Association. [Addresses the issue of linguistic sexism in scholarly and professional writing, presenting relevant ideas and research and excellent guidelines for nondiscriminatory usage.]

Freelance Editors' Association of Canada. 1987. "Avoiding Bias." In *Editing Canadian English*, pp. 87–100. Vancouver/Toronto: Douglas McIntyre. [Brief, useful guidelines, with hard-to-find advice for writing about sexual orientation and disabilities and including some nuances for editing in a Canadian context.]

Longyear, Marie, ed. 1983. "Bias-Free Publishing." In *The McGraw-Hill Style Manual: A Concise Guide for Writers and Editors*, pp. 272–84. New York: McGraw-Hill. [A stan-

dard style manual offering excellent guidelines for bias-
free writing; racism and sexism are treated extensively
and handicapism and ageism briefly.]

Maggio, Rosalie. 1991. *The Bias-Free Word Finder: A Dictionary
of Nondiscriminatory Language*. Boston: Beacon Press. [An
expanded edition of *The Nonsexist Word Finder,* an excellent resource, though terms are insufficiently cross referenced for convenient use.]

——. 1989. *The Nonsexist Word Finder: A Dictionary of Gender-Free Usage*. Boston: Beacon Press. [Excellent, exten-
sive dictionary of problematic terms, from "abbess" to
"youth," including many troublesome set phrases (e.g.,
"man for all seasons"), with usage recommendations;
contains a foreword by Casey Miller and Kate Swift,
appendixes of writing guidelines and brief readings, and
a bibliography. The most complete usage glossary available and an essential reference for editors.]

Miller, Casey, and Kate Swift. 1988. *The Handbook of Nonsexist
Writing: For Writers, Editors, and Speakers,* 2d ed. New
York: Harper and Row. [Originally published in 1980,
this essential paperback handbook has now been reis-
sued with a brief thesaurus of gender-free terms, revisions of troublesome maxims, and a list of inclusive
language resources for religious worship.]

National Easter Seal Society. [1986]. *Portraying People with
Disabilities in the Media*. [Chicago]. [Nine-page booklet
includes guidelines for discussing people with disabilities
and a glossary of preferred terms describing disabilities.
Publication no. PR-43, available from the National Easter Seal Society, 2023 W. Ogden Ave., Chicago, IL
60612.]

National Organization for Women. n.d. *Practical Guide to
Non-Sexist Language*. St. Louis, MO. [Two-sided flyer of
recommended usages, handy as a brief style sheet for
authors and others requesting guidance in brief form.

Available from South and West St. Louis County Chapter, National Organization for Women, 1025 Barry Court, St. Louis, MO 63122.]

Pickens, Judy E., ed. 1982. *Without Bias: A Guidebook for Nondiscriminatory Communication,* 2d ed. New York: John Wiley and Sons. [Straightforward advice for verbal and nonverbal communication free of bias with regard to race, sex, disability, or age; a bit too general for university press publishing.]

Research and Training Center on Independent Living. 1984. *Guidelines for Reporting and Writing about People with Disabilities.* Lawrence, KS. [Short flyer containing useful advice about general issues and specific terminology. Available from the Media Project, Research and Training Center on Independent Living, 348 Haworth Hall, University of Kansas, Lawrence, KS 66045.]

Sorrels, Bobbye D. 1983. *The Nonsexist Communicator: Solving the Problems of Gender and Awkwardness in Modern English.* Englewood Cliffs, NJ: Prentice-Hall/Spectrum Books. [Organized for text use in communications workshops. Good exposition and usage guide, with (sometimes overdrawn) examples, exercises, and answer section; includes a substantial glossary of alternatives to sexist terms.]

Index